PARADISE PARKWAY

BAZ THA NOMAD

PARADISE PARKWAY

A SELF-HELP JOURNEY OF MAKING OUR DREAMS COME TRUE

H.A.P.P.Y. BOOKS

A Home Alone Productions Company

Copyright © 2021 by Home Alone Productions, LLC

Published by H.A.P.P.Y. BOOKS: A Home Alone Productions Company

Illustrated by Baz Tha Nomad © 2021

All rights reserved. Printed in the United States of America. No part of this may be used or reproduced in any manner whatsoever without written permission except in the case of brief quotations embodied in critical articles or reviews.

This is a work of fiction. Although its form is that of an autobiography, it is not one. Space and time have been rearranged to suit the convenience of the book, and with the exception of public figures, any resemblance to persons living or dead is coincidental. The opinions expressed are those of the characters and should not be confused with the author's.

Library of Congress Cataloging-in-Publication Data has been applied for.

ISBN: 978-1-7371511-0-4 (paperback)
ISBN: 978-1-7371511-1-1 (ebook)
ISBN: 978-1-7371511-2-8 (hardback)

*To You,
The one that was called to pick this book.
May my thoughts and experiences be the story you needed to hear in order to step into your true strength.
I love you dearly. Thank You.*

- Baz Tha Nomad

Now, shall we begin?

TABLE OF CONTENTS

I. Introduction | *1*

II. Fear | *9*

III. Confidence | *24*

IV. Insanity | *39*

V. Addiction | *54*

VI. Diet | *70*

VII. Company | *81*

VIII. Patience | *94*

IX. Love | *109*

X. Priorities | *122*

XI. You | *135*

Chapter One

INTRODUCTION

"Oh, the Places You'll Go!" - Dr. Seuss

Oh, blah blah blah, how many times have you heard that quote? Every time, it gets more irritating because the toxic optimism in it never runs out. Although positivity can help inspire someone to keep pushing forward, it doesn't take away any of the pain, obstacles, or traumatic experiences people face while they are on their journey. It only negates any safe space they have for how they feel, leaving them with no choice but to ignore them and continue pushing forward until they completely burn out and have no more fight left in them. But that isn't the most effective way of going about it; trust me, I would know.

As intellectual beings with the power to act upon our own thoughts, it's our sole responsibility to acknowledge and nurture how we think and feel on an internal level. Our level of mental stamina and emotional intelligence dictates the speed and quality of our progression. With more fear than confidence, one can fall ten steps backward when in reality it could've been three steps ahead, if only they overcame that obstacle the first time it came around three years ago (this got a little personal, I know). But it's the truth! We tend to get so caught up with the "just keep going" attitude that we forget that we need rest and reorganizing in order to not drive us insane. People can always say it's as easy as taking that first step, but from the outside looking in, do they even understand how hard it is for that first step alone? And then the next one, and the one following that?

Many of us don't have the proper guidance, peers, or sheer wisdom to properly execute what needs to be done while also finding time to be kind to ourselves. When's the last time you had a bubble bath? Took yourself on a date? Played oldie's music to clean your room while performing your own dance routine? How long have you been cheating yourself from the best version of yourself because you just didn't know any better? It's okay to be honest with

Chapter One

yourself; in fact, it's where we need to start to see actual results.

For those of you who haven't guessed by now, yes, this is yet another self-help "YOU CAN DO IT" book to read when you're feeling shitty about the shitty outcomes of shitty situations you put yourself in to begin with. OR you can be somebody who's gone through something totally out of your control and just keeps looking for the right words that'll help make sense out of what happened. Either way you look at it —

coughs

WELCOME TO PARADISE PARKWAY! THE ROAD WHERE THERE'LL ALWAYS BE ANOTHER BLOODY OBSTACLE AROUND THE CORNER! WHERE FEAR FEEDS BOTH THE FUEL AND THE MONSTERS! WHERE CHASING THE END OF THE TUNNEL WILL LEAD YOU DOWN A RABBIT HOLE LIKE NO OTHER! COME ONE! COME ALL! A JOURNEY MEANT FOR EVERY ONE OF US!

Now, doesn't that sound enticing? Of course, it doesn't! Who wants to go through hell to get to paradise? Why can't it be as simple as closing your eyes, putting your hands together and asking God, "Can I have a billion dollars?" Why must our trophies be at the far end of a treacherous path? Why can't we get a second to breathe before the next crisis comes about? WHY?

The answer's pretty simple. Most of us ignore the truth because we'd honestly rather complain or struggle and evidently stay stagnant because we became comfortable with our current circumstances. Before reading further, I want you to take a second to figure out what it is. Put down the book if you need to. Trust me, there are no wrong answers here, only a variety of opinions that 99% of the time will relate back to the one truth. A truth so powerful, it can be implemented in every aspect of this Universe, yet be described in one word.

Balance.

Chapter One

Left and right. North and south. Good and bad. Pain and joy. Clean and dirty. Light and dark. Angels and demons. Sun and Moon. Love and war. Woman and man. What would any of these things be without the other? How would we even know what something is without comparing it with what it isn't? How would we know what a dirty room looked like without ever knowing what a clean room was? How would we know about the Moon without it appearing in the Sun's absence?

How do you experience everything you've ever wanted in life without going through everything to get to that point? It's simple; you don't. This poetic nature is something our Creator instilled in us down to the molecular level. We cherish life so much because we know we eventually die. We eat healthily and stay fit (or do the complete opposite) to feel better about how we lived. We'll chase after that love because we feel as if they are the one we want to spend our last moments with. And like it or not, all of this is hard fucking work. Commitment on top of dedication with a side of self-empowerment in case the determination is running low, type of work. There are no shortcuts, cheat codes, or any amount of people that can/will do this work for you if it's something that YOU want. The Universe rewards those that set their intention of acquiring something and take actions that place them closer to what it is they want to achieve. Nobody said it would be easy, and everybody said it's worth it, but can you really believe it until you experience it yourself?

I'm here to tell you that you're not alone, because I'm in the same sinking boat with you, believe it or not. Actually, writing this book is a way for me to process everything I'm dealing with so that I don't fade into an endless pattern of depression. I'm tired of feeling like this. I'm tired of working so hard to make progress, only to let one small thing knock me down back to level one. I deserve consistency. I deserve to be kind to myself when things don't look like they're going in my favor. I deserve a warm, comforting hug and a "you're doing great, my love" for maintaining the determination to keep pushing forward.

Chapter One

And so do you. We all deserve the reassurance and guidance that we crave, and we should never feel ashamed to admit we want these things. We're all human. We all have emotions and a sense of belonging to somewhere, someone, something. We all do. Those who deny this are trying to stay strong so their own ego doesn't shatter from an overload of neglected shadow work. Don't be this person. We aren't going to get along much during this journey if you keep that front up.

I am EMOTIONAL. Passion is my element! It's where I grab inspiration to be a better version of myself, as well as the purest expression in my art. I believe to live doing what you're passionate about is life's true purpose, so here I am! Passionately writing a book about becoming passionate in the treacherous journey everyone must undergo in order to let their passions flourish to their max potential. And while confiding my vulnerability in each one of you readers, I hope that you can take my story, experiences, and perspective to find a way to implement the lessons and tips they teach into your daily lives, making you into the prestige version of yourself that you always knew you were! If nobody reads this, then I can still say that I was aware enough to break down the aspects that have greatly affected my uprisings and downfalls.

And I made them into A WHOLE BOOK.

Starting as a carefree soul growing up, I would have never thought I'd get myself to really write a book, let alone a self-help book about MY mental health. This is my step forward into my life's purpose, and I thank you for acknowledging the importance of mental health awareness and being interested enough about my thoughts that you've made it this far, the end of the first chapter. I love you more than these black and white words can describe, and I want you to know that I'm so glad that you've decided to take this journey with me.

We'll grow together, we'll make our mistakes together, and whenever I feel like things are getting overwhelming or off track, I'll turn to this book and continue writing so you can then turn to my words

Chapter One

when things get overwhelming in your life. I got your back; you got mine. Got it? Good!

Let's begin!

* Where's Dora when you need her most? *

FEAR

"Tell your heart that the fear of suffering is worse than the fear itself." - Paulo Coelho, The Alchemist

Anyone who has been around me for a while will know how much I'm obsessed with *The Alchemist*. If you haven't read it just yet, then I'm probably going to ruin it for you, but one piece of advice I have is don't force yourself to read it if it isn't time (but you might want to put this book down until you do). What I got from it was that it's about a boy's journey to find out his true purpose in this world; where he can be content with the values he's already established, or he can face his fears and allow himself to be open to all the signs the Universe is giving him.

Throughout this journey, he faces challenges he would have never experienced if he had never taken that first step, and the next one, and the one after that. The whole time, this boy makes mistakes, faces detours, finds friends, and digs deeper within himself to achieve his Soul's Purpose. Even if achieving his

Chapter Two

goal meant going through a certain level of suffering, he was aware of it from the beginning. He knew that taking that leap of faith would mean leaving his old job, values, lover, and even his old self in the past. He knew that this brand-new start sounded impossible to the average person. So, why did he even take that first step?

Well (like ALWAYS), it started off as a dream. A dream he could not decipher on his own, so he sought help from someone he wouldn't usually go to, a gypsy. His dream seeped into his subconscious with such depth that he needed to understand why it was reoccurring. Although he had his doubts about this not being real, let alone obtainable, the Universe kept on nudging him to drop everything and follow that dream. Now, for those of you who've already read the story (which I hope is all of you at this point), you know the irony of where the story ends. All I'll say is as long as you follow the signs given to you, you'll always find yourself at the right place at the right time, no matter the circumstances.

Think about it like this; would you have rather loved and lost than never loved at all? Some would say the latter, and I will tell them they are foolish! In my life, I've fallen in and out of love a few times, and at the very least, I can say, "What an experience!" Even if it didn't work out for whatever reason, the experience as a whole is something I can appreciate and grow from after it's over. I've learned more from being vulnerable and putting myself out there than I ever did staying afraid of any type of intimacy or connection. Although I wish my love life didn't crumble to pieces (like a lot of us), I've realized that experiencing the mistakes, the faults, the joy, and the euphoria is what really taught me what it is that I want, as well as do not want, in my life.

Without putting myself out there, I'd limit myself from all the character development that happened throughout the process. How can you know what you want in a person if you never experience what you don't want? Accepting that fear only leaves room to daydream and contemplate what could be or why you must not be worthy or good enough to have such a feeling in your life, which isn't true at all.

Chapter Two

Everyone deserves to have love in their life. Everyone deserves to pursue whatever it is that makes them genuinely happy. The only thing that genuinely stops them is fear; fear of failure, fear of rejection, fear of death, fear of basically anything imaginable. People don't want to achieve their highest potential because they're afraid that it won't be easy, or they'll have to let go of specific attachments or obsessions of their current life. Whether it be habits, people, environment, or maybe even their physical attributes, fear is what stops them from taking that step into the unknown.

That's the beauty of it, though! Once you conquer your fear and take that first step, EVERYTHING that comes next is an outcome you couldn't have seen. Usually, there are some bumps in the road that'll delay your progress or even bump you down a level or two. This isn't a sign to panic and listen to that voice you have already begun to ignore; this is the beauty of the journey. True progression towards our Soul's Purpose will rarely be linear. It'll be more like a stock market chart where it continuously fluctuates from all-time highs to all-time lows, leaving the participants on a constant emotional rollercoaster. However, this doesn't mean you cash out when things get tough. The main lesson I learned in stocks is to sell high and buy low.

Now bringing it back full circle (because I know you're probably confused from that tangent—don't worry, you'll get used to it), when life knocks you down to a new all-time low, does that mean you should give up and accept the minimum given to you? Of course not. It means you double down and put even more investment into it because you know it has the utmost potential to move in a positive direction. Now I'm not giving you stock advice, so please don't lose your savings by irresponsibly investing. I'm merely talking in metaphors (one of my favorite ways of getting the point across). When you're invested in something in your life, it's very apparent that you want to see the best results possible, and when things are looking good, it feels amazing. But it's those plummets that truly test how devoted you are to see that end goal.

Chapter Two

That feeling of fear is honestly one of the most challenging obstacles in my life for the simple fact that it's not real! The amount of fear felt is based on how much attention I give that feeling, evidently validating its reason to be there and fueling the flame even more. The scary part about it is that, again, fear isn't real. It's not something you can measure with a ruler or thermometer, but an emotion that initially starts as a thought. Just like you can't say, "Today I am 300 grams of happiness," you can't pinpoint the amount of fear you feel. You can only acknowledge the fact that it's there and do your best to not feed it. The moment you do, it'll then try to trick you into a rabbit hole that'll convince you how real the fear is until you allow it to dictate what you do in this reality.

There were plenty of times in my youth when I wouldn't approach a girl out of the fear of overall rejection. Whether I'd say the wrong thing, fumble my words, seem awkward, or say something downright foolish, the feeling fed me all these potentially embarrassing scenarios to stop me from failure. But if I listened to them, let alone any fear I've ever had, I would've ended up a very antisocial, undeveloped individual that felt sorry for himself. Needless to say, neither of those resonate with who I am, nor who I want to become, so it was imperative that I learned how to fight these fears. If I wasn't so devoted to my growth, I wouldn't even be making this book for all of us. I've always been fearful about sharing my thoughts, opinions, and life story with others because I feel like I'm being judged for how vulnerable I am in such a cold-hearted world. Even now, as I'm writing these words, I've had to put on some sound healing meditation music for background noise just to help drown out the side chatter my fears are having in my head.

"Am I writing too much? Am I making sense, or am I all over the place? Am I writing in a way that keeps the readers' attention? Is this something people would actually read? Am I wasting my time? Do people even really care enough to even pick up a book like this, let alone read it front to back? What if I spent all this time just for it to flop? Are people going to make fun of me because I'm open up about my mental health? Is my story going to help or hinder someone dealing with similar issues? Am I even qualified to be an author? Is anyone really going to take my intellect seriously, even if I'm a college dropout? Are people going to accept my multidimensional creative outlets? Am I writing this book for only selfish reasons, like profit? What was the point of even starting this? Is there a point of even finishing it?"

Trust me, I could keep going if this was a book about listening to your self-doubt. The point is, my own fear is something I battle with on a daily basis, but it's no longer something I let dictate my life. Each day it gets easier to handle, not because the fear goes away, but because I prove to myself that I can transmute it with each passing moment. If I could do it in my past, that means the same can be done today and every day that comes after.

Each chapter in this book took me quite some time to formulate, organize, draft, and edit, and I'd like to take the time to recognize my efforts to get through this chapter alone. I've had to dig deep into the entirety of this craft in order to pinpoint and analyze all my fears and find the root issue for each one, and then apply the tactics I saw that could help both my personal fears as well as yours, my beloved reader. Before continuing, I just want to reiterate that you should be kind to yourself during this process. Just by taking the time to read this, you're playing a part in not just your growth; you're playing your role in the collective's ascension.

Remember, this is something that can't be rushed; it'll never be instantaneous. If I could gather the Infinity Stones and Thanos-snap my fingers to achieve my goal, I would. But this process requires recognizing the issue, unlearning the behavior, and then reteaching yourself a more suitable way to experience the emotion. This is NOT an overnight thing. For me, it's been six months since I recognized the root of my fear, and I'm still actively working on it. So, be patient. At first, I talked myself out of writing this chapter, let alone this entire book, day in and day out, and I almost listened. I almost killed myself because I felt like I wasn't smart enough, attractive enough, or strong enough to use my voice for such an elite purpose like this. But again, here I am, delivering each word with the faith that it can change someone's life for the better, not just mine. I believe in you.

The trickiest part here is, well, I don't know you. All I have is the results from the research and surveys I've conducted to gain the knowledge necessary to speak on these things. But still, there's a high chance that I didn't get the time to talk to you specifically. And for that, I'm going to stick to a more generic approach to providing support. Funny enough, one of my fears right now is the possibility of me not covering every corner and failing to shine light onto your individual fear.

Don't laugh! It's my truth! People can have the silliest of fears! The trick I found is to analyze all of them in black and white. So, whether you're afraid of a simple apocalypse or something more complex, like not helping others conquer their fears, you can apply this black and white outline to whatever it is! Just be sure to add its respective color to personalize your path to success. The last thing we want is you being afraid of mice yet jumping out of a plane because that's how someone else faced their fear of heights. ALWAYS do and apply what resonates with you.

You Vs. Fear

First things first, we have to define what fear is to you. I know it may seem silly at first, but acknowledging it is the most important part! If you're not aware of what it is, how do you expect to figure out why you have this feeling? Don't worry too much about the "why" just yet; that'll happen in the steps to come. If it helps, the more textbook definition is "an unpleasant emotion caused by the belief that something is dangerous or a threat." What are some things that make you feel this way?

Some common fears would be heights, animals, water, failure, divorce, aging, making mistakes, losing a loved one, new environments, the unknown; trust me, the list goes on. List out all the things, big or small, that cause your fear to grow. Be sure to list EVERYTHING. Don't let the randomness or silliness of what comes out discourage this process. Think of yourself as an artist, and this the freestyle draft to creating your life's masterpiece. Take some time to self-reflect, but don't overthink it!

Got your list filled out? Great! Now it's time to find the root of your fear. It's been proven that fear isn't something we're born with; it's learned behavior. It usually stems from things from our childhood or our past in general. So, our mission here is to figure out what that is exactly. Take some time at this stage to meditate with your Root Chakra.

For those of you who are new to this form of spiritual practice, this is the spherical energy center of your vessel residing at the base of your spine. It's the fuel for our primal instincts, like safety, strength, responsibility, survival, and sense of who we are. Whenever we feel fear, it's derived from instabilities in this chakra. Exploit this! Use the list you've made to give you some hints as to what it is you're terrified of.

Sometimes when someone has a fear of heights, birds, and new experiences, it could be a result of something along the lines of being attacked by pigeons right at the peak of their first roller coaster climb. Sounds oddly specific and unique, doesn't it? Good, take it as comic relief. You'll be surprised when you figure out the source of your fear. Some may be hilarious when you look back on it, while others can be pretty triggering to bring back up to the surface. Remember to be kind to yourself.

Now that you've truly defined both the size and depth of your pool of fears, it's time to jump in! It's as easy as cannonballing into the deep end and figuring it out from there for some people. For others, they have to start by dipping their big toe in first and then gradually stepping in as they acclimate to this sensation. Do what works best for you! Don't do what worked best for others! Their route may have gotten them where you want to be, but there can be another path with a more pleasing scenery to your goal if you just take the time to look for yourself.

Step by step. Brick by brick. Day by day. These are mantras you'll hear me say more and more as you pay closer attention. I know how scary it feels to be stuck in your own mental prison. As much as I wanted to karate kick the bars of fear and escape in a cool, heroic fashion, that's not what happened. It happened after repeating daily affirmations to remind myself I had the power to take control of my life. It happened after facing my fears with an inch more courage than I had the last time. It happened after I realized that there's strength in being present in the moment rather than stuck in my head. It happened after I forgave myself for not reaching completion and congratulated the amount of progress gained. It happened after having faith that it was a learning experience for me to evolve. It happened after I did these things every single day. Every. Single. Day.

 Speaking from experience, I can assure you that I've experienced more progress moving at my own pace than I ever did trying to match someone else's. My personal scenic route has led me to not only conquering any fears and doubts I had before, but to opportunities I once thought only happened in movies. Now my life IS a movie (well, not an actual movie just yet, but that's in the works).

Also, I hope you don't share my fear of asking for help, because a support system is one hell of a life preserver here. Look for a loved one to confide your feelings in, or even go to your therapist! Don't have one? GET ONE. They'll do a marvelous job at helping unravel the unique solution you're searching for.

Recap: Just breath. Remember you have the strength to face your fears, and it's absolutely okay to move at your own pace. One day, you'll be doing laps around your pool of fears.

Journaling Topic Question: What really makes your fears scary? Is this a limitation you're willing to accept for yourself?

Chapter Three

CONFIDENCE

"Confidence is contagious, so is lack of confidence." - Vince Lombardi

When you think of confidence, what do you see? I asked my uncle and aunt (mainly because they are sitting next to me) to spark some inspiration, and their answers were; assertiveness and Tom Brady, respectively. This made me smile since the quote chosen for this topic is from the man who has the Super Bowl trophy named after him. This brought to my attention that even though there is a textbook definition for it, everyone has their own unique way of tapping into or recognizing it. Kind of like how we can look at a very unorthodox chair yet know it's a type of seat; we're able to acknowledge what it's portraying because we know what it's supposed to look like.

So, when it comes to confidence, I found it hard to talk about for two reasons. For starters, I couldn't get myself to define it in my own terms instead of running to Google, which caused a massive amount of writer's block. Whenever I tried to spitball something out, my attempt of empowerment completely lacked the concept of confidence. It was like I was telling you the flames don't burn while you're watching my skin evaporate off of my bones. Or like telling you to dive face-first while water filled my lungs. That's when it hit me; the reason I couldn't write about confidence was because that was what I'd been missing.

As I wrote my way through this growth process, most of it was a combination of me recognizing the parts of me I wanted to improve and accepting them as they were to implement real change. Talking about myself was easy! Each entry was my own self-therapy sessions where I was free to vent and feel listened to (even if nobody else was reading it at that moment). The real challenge came when I finished addressing my issues and I had to actually walk the walk that I was talking about, the same journey I hope you're taking.

Throughout my life, I always knew what I wanted, I was just never sure that I was on the most effective path to get it, and it showed. I can say with confidence that I used to be an embodiment of my lack of confidence. I had a plethora of different things left incomplete, dabbled in habits that never aligned with my highest self, and would barely post no-filter pictures on social media. Yet, here I wanted to tell everyone that they should believe in themselves. That they should love themselves correctly because they're already beautiful. That they're already enough. As much as I wanted to grasp their attention and help shed light on their darkest moments, I came to the understanding that I was not waving, but drowning. And if I spoke from a place of drowning while trying to influence others, I could have very well led many people to the same sinking place I was in.

Here's an opinion of mine that's helped me stay so dedicated in pursuing what makes ME happy and not anyone else; nobody knows what they're doing. I'll repeat it once more. NOBODY KNOWS WHAT THEY'RE DOING.

How many of you can say you were born and were already in the know? That no matter what you did or saw or experienced, you already knew what would happen? Even if we've tapped into our spirit and realized we've lived many lives before this one, it's a part of the sacred reincarnation process to wipe all the memories of those lives. That way, we have a fresh start in our next try at life.

I don't want to confuse you by going off on another tangent. I just want to get the point across that nobody has the answers. Everyone only has a sense of what the answer should be, and that itself is based on their wisdom from their own experiences. It's become a regular practice to lean on what the collective agrees with because we aren't sure enough to even have our own opinion. So, when everyone tells you to stop chasing your dreams as a rockstar because it's not a guaranteed route to financial stability, you need to be able to recognize that they're saying this because their uncertainty in the unknown is greater than their faith in what can be.

Chapter Three

This is where confidence plays a significant role in our lives. When you're confident, it means you're unwaveringly certain in whatever the topic is. No amount of doubt, criticism, or force can stop you because that unshakable faith allows you to stride forward while slicing through any obstacle in the way. Usually, the people who embody this confidence have spent countless amounts of time and energy gaining endless knowledge and perfecting their practice. They know that by putting so much effort into making sure there was no stone left unturned, they've minimized their chances of failure.

Now, hear me out! I'm not saying that being confident guarantees that you won't experience failure; I'm saying that confidence can help you accept a long, bumpy road towards success. Actually, having confidence that you'll succeed will probably bring about more challenging experiences. It'll influence you to dive headfirst in some pretty scary situations. A perfect phrase to describe this would be "no guts, no glory."

Most successful people know that reaching resistance is only the necessary training one must go through to truly be "fit" to hold up the trophy at the finish line. I say "most" because, well, not everyone goes through this process. Some people have the trophy handed to them on a silver platter where they probably have no idea what it took to obtain the prize. Some people will be intimidated by the roller coaster that comes with striving towards the top and will try to find a shortcut to avoid the obstacles they deem unnecessary. I believe it's human nature to look at the last two and think, "Damn, they got it easy. Why I gotta struggle to move up each step when they're breezing by without breaking a sweat?" Trust me, I've had the same thoughts before. It wasn't until I realized that all the tedious obstacles I've conquered before are what truly prepared me for the "boss battle" that stood between me and my grand prize.

You see, being able to say, "I almost thought I wouldn't make it, but look at me! I really did it!" is a very simple phrase that many will laugh at, but winners will praise. When looking at anyone's end result, you can clearly see the reward presented to

Chapter Three

them for reaching that point. But how did they get it, exactly? Did they cheat their way to the top? Did they find the easy way out? Or did they fail, again and again, trying to overcome the journey, yet got back up every time and finally reached their goal?

In the end, the cheater, the gifted, and the determined can all achieve their end goal (don't get the wrong idea, keep reading). But who do you think is the happiest? Who do you think REALLY knows they're successful? The cheater will always be carefree until they're caught, forcing their prize to be revoked and left to struggle to earn it correctly. The gifted will be pleased with their award because that's all they wanted. That's the reason that they participated in the first place. Now, what if the prize isn't what they desire? More than likely, they'll lose their motivation to achieve greatness again because they'll think their effort isn't worth the end result. They'll slack off because they believe they're the best, and that prize, whether it be a trophy or a career or whatever, will always be there for them whenever they decide to try. They'll even blame the process for their shortcomings if they experience some resistance on their path. Though they possess extreme talent in their field, those gifted individuals are the readers that I want to convert into the Determined.

The Determined is the individual that accepts their humanity. They do not accept failure, yet they come to terms with the fact that it is a part of the process they are on. The phrase "fall down nine times but stand up ten" would be perfect for this individual. They look at obstacles with a sense of determination because they know that it's merely that, an obstacle. Something that's meant to be conquered on their path; something that can strike fear into their heart if they don't stand firm in their self-beliefs and values. This drive for success helps them reflect on their failures and strategically learn from past mistakes to find the correct formula for the problem. It's this determination that makes them appreciate the growth that occurred during the journey, which in the end puts more value into the prize received at the finish line. They look at the prize and not only see the end accomplishment, but all the mini ones that had to be achieved to even qualify for the end prize.

Chapter Three

    Now, a lot of you will probably bring up the fact that if the Gifted is gifted enough, then they'll never fail, but that's not even true in fairy tales. In shows and movies that we all love, the main character usually starts as one of the Gifted. Talented and carefree, yet close-minded to the bigger picture. Throughout whatever story it is (and believe me, almost every hero's story ties this lesson into it somewhere), that character experiences a challenge that they cannot overcome, sending them multiple levels down to where it seems they're back at square one. Now since they are at a new low point, the gifted have a decision to make; whether they will accept the fate given to them and give up on what they once wanted, or go through retraining their perspective of things. Instead of feeling like they are deserving and worthy of what they want by just being, they switch their values into diving into the process head-on with the determination that they'll see that obstacle again one day, and when that time comes, they'll be ready.

"Hard work beats talent when talent fails to work hard."

The Eye of the Tiger

Bom! Bom Bom Bom! Bom Bom Bom! Bom Bom Bommmmmmmmm!!!!!! It's one thing to hope for the best. It's another to KNOW the best is coming. Having confidence requires a firm trust in something, whether it be the outcome of a sports game, the results of a test, or even as simple as the words that you say. It means that no fear, doubt, or opinion can influence/waver your stance because you KNOW. You don't think you know, you KNOW.

Some people have a natural self-confidence instilled in them by their parents, which is PHENOMENAL. Others, like me, have had a history of people tearing them down and crushing their dreams which led to unfortunate self-doubt that is way too popular nowadays. But understand that's okay! All this means is that you get to skip a step that the self-confident readers might have to undergo, even though it may seem like they're already a step ahead. That step is humbling yourself.

Chapter Three

There's a fine line between confidence and arrogance. As much as I would love to talk about confidence as the sure-fire way to solve all your problems, it's wise to remind ourselves that we're only human. Nobody has all the answers, or at least from my experiences, that's what I've witnessed. No matter how high and mighty someone can appear, they are still subject to making a mistake like any one of us. The best solution to avoid this is to stay knowledgeable in what you want to be confident in.

Want to jump into sporting arguments with the homies? Look up recent stats, watch all the games, spend your free time on ESPN or listening to podcasts. Want to get in better shape? Do some research and find a meal plan that works for you! Find exercises that isolate the areas you really want to work on. Want to create a multidimensional project that contains multiple fields you've never pursued before? You better spend all your time not only studying the best in each craft, but practicing as much as you can so that you can make progress in achieving the desired results. Think about your scholar days when it was time for your finals; what made you the most confident that you were going to ace it? Was it when all semester you completed the assignments, spent countless sleepless nights going over the material, and even made yourself your very own study guide? Or was it when you were slacking off, skipping class to see your significant other, and prioritizing winning in Fortnite over getting that college credit?

    I'm not here saying it isn't possible to go down the second route and still achieve your desired results; I'm saying you can feel the difference in confidence both students have after their exam. The factor of lacking knowledge can easily lead to uncertainty and, ultimately, a lack of confidence. So, whatever it is you want (clearer skin, performing on stage, start an OnlyFans, etc.), make sure you do the work to really understand what you're supposed to be doing in that field and implement it! Be that determined individual who takes their shortcomings as a learning experience for growth, not as another failure while attempting success. Stay humble and always be teachable so you stay at the top of your game.

Chapter Three

Some things that have really helped me with my own confidence are my daily affirmations; every time I wake up and again before going to sleep. I'll list them for you, but I encourage you to personalize one that establishes what traits you'd like to embrace. In the beginning, I'd sometimes forget to recite them before opening my eyes and picking up my phone and noticed myself reverting back to old thought patterns, so stay disciplined.

Set up a self-care routine and stick to it! Consistency in things like working out, dressing up, maintaining hygiene, and journaling are long-term ways to gain real, unwavering confidence (emphasis on journaling). If you can be vulnerable with yourself about what you lack confidence in, then you can figure out the steps you should take by simply letting the words flow out. You know you best; it's just so hard sometimes when the infinite number of thoughts don't have a place to go other than swim around like a goldfish in its fishbowl.

Plus, if you know you, not only the faults but your strengths too, then there's nothing anyone can tell you about yourself! Especially when you've reached the long-term effects of staying consistent. At that point, you realize any attempts to kick you off your high horse are caused by the attacker's own lack of confidence. All you can do is pity them and know you're always protected.

To practice this during meditation, allow your attention to focus on your solar plexus. This chakra is responsible for self-empowerment, courage, freedom, and identity, perfect for channeling our inner strength. From experience, I can say that during this process, I noticed a lot of hurt that I had to heal before energy could flow freely, so understand it's a process that'll require you to be kind to yourself in case old trauma comes back up. But again, it is truly worth going through.

My Affirmations: I am Worthy, I am Capable, I am Willing, I am Love, I am Light, I am Forgiving, I am Understanding, I am Compassionate, I am Human, I am Unapologetically Me. Asé.

Journaling Topic Question: Who am I at my most powerful? How can I commit to waking up as that person every day?

INSANITY

"The definition of insanity is to do the same thing over and over again and expect different results." - Not Albert Einstein

I'd like to start by saying this is a quote I've heard countless times and never knew its origin. I've heard it in shows, came across it in conversation, and never did anyone credit the person who spoke such wisdom. Obviously, if I talked about it in this book, I had to do my own research because, well, talking about it without acknowledging where it's from just seems unethical. What I found time and time again was an answer that was so unsatisfying it almost drove me insane, ironically.

"Not Albert Einstein."

Excuse me but… what? It MIGHT be Mark Twain? But no one is sure? You mean to tell me everyone can talk about how people famously mistake it as Einstein's words but can't back it with solid evidence of where it's from?

Fuck it, I digress.

Who here has ever caught themselves practicing insanity? Ever had dreams of becoming a professional athlete and thought the amount of work you put in was adequate enough to get you there? Maybe wanted to sing like Beyonce but never took the time to train your voice consistently to get it there?

The point is, we can all get delusional sometimes and believe that what we're doing is an effective way to get where we want to be, even when we already played that hand before and got underwhelming results. Think about a stalker who believes one day you'll love them even after you rejected them repeatedly. It could be triggering, I know, but hopefully, I got the point across.

To tell you a little about myself, I am an artist that expresses my life stories through my multiple crafts. Whether it be music, graphic designing, or even writing, I try to make sure what's presented is an accurate representation of who I am and what I've gone through. I've always been filled with pure joy ever since I was young. It's just, the experiences I've been through have always tried to steal that feeling away from me. From my family, friends, to even my intimate relationships, I've dealt with specific patterns that I didn't overcome the first time, so they eventually came back around later in life. Whether it be pertaining to the same people or just the devil in a new dress, this was a source of my insanity.

    My problem was, even though I was witty enough to acknowledge something like a repeated pattern, my final action/reaction would almost unconsciously mirror what happened in the past, leading to the same dreadful, lonely experiences that followed after. Due to my awareness of this constant loop, my overall health started to plummet; dropping from an already underweight 120 all the way down to 105 (I'm six feet tall, by the way, so just imagine the lankiness). I felt abandoned by my "loved ones" and neglected by the love of my life (at the time). I constantly replayed the scenarios in my head and beat myself up about receiving the same undesirable result as before.

I realized that even though I'd been through it before, I had not correctly healed or even understood my mistakes! I only suppressed my trauma and emotions with constant highs like narcotics or over-giving myself to others, which led to short-term happiness where I would be numb for a brief period. That's when I would feel those inescapable depressing thoughts creep back in as the highs faded away, unfortunately influencing me to indulge in more to stay away from fixing my real personal issues.

As a result, here I am today, currently writing back at square one (yet again) with a freshly removed wisdom tooth and a sober mind. Not only do I wish I could say that I handled recent patterns efficiently this time, I wish I could say that last time was the last time I experience such a situation. But I'd be lying to myself. I know this will reoccur until I can reflect on the deeper issue and deal with it in the correct manner that the Universe is trying to teach me.

Dealing with repeated issues can be extremely draining and discouraging. I don't think it's something anyone wants to go through. Achieving the same unsettling results every time? That can drive almost anyone insane! Everyone, no matter your race, gender, sexuality, is on a journey that will have obstacles and pitfalls created to distract you from the feeling of climbing to the top of the mountain.

We can get so wrapped up in the moment that our immediate response is to do what was done last time we were in a similar situation. It's like fight or flight. It's engraved in our brain to react a certain way to specific circumstances. Maybe we absorbed it from childhood, or perhaps we developed it ourselves throughout the years of past success, so now it's our go-to method. Anytime we face a problem, it can feel like the one and only lightbulb that turns on in our head, so instinctively, we can jump the gun and turn to it (think of "Fear of Missing Out").

Chapter Three

In your experience, has that worked out well so far? Has it gotten you the actual results you expected from your choice, time and time again? If so, then bravo! You have better luck than me. Feel free to put this book down and write your own because I would LOVE to read how you've reached pinnacle success with your method. Until then, I'll keep writing.

I'm just honest with myself! There is no way in hell you can tell me that in this life we live, I can make the same singular choice in any situation and get the desired result. The only exception I'll accept is if I want the same result an infinite amount of times. But even still, life is constantly changing. Our environment is always changing. WE are changing.

Let me exaggerate it like this: If you go to the vending machine, do you get the same thing every single time? If you do, you probably have it in your head that you're paying one dollar in exchange for your favorite snack. Every time you happily walk down the hall knowing what's about to happen. You're going to put your dollar in, press A8, and—wait, why is the metal spring still keeping grandma's cookies captive? You did everything right. It's not like it was calculus; it was a very simple formula. Dollar, code, snack. It's been done so many times that you can do it with your eyes closed. So why? That's when you look at the tiny rectangle screen and realize they put a tax on grandma's cookies. Instead of one dollar, it's now a dollar and fifty cents.

Like it or not, nothing stays the same. We're born, grow, and then die. Even things like water constantly change forms naturally every single day. So, don't be so hard-headed and think you can be the singularity that can defy nature and forcefully break the barrier. Instead, think of a different form of what it is you're doing.

Can't get your kid to open up by using forceful tactics? How about taking some time to try learning what situations or environment makes them comfortable enough to talk to you about what's on their mind. Can you never take vacations because you never have the money? Get a job! Stop spending all the money that you do have on frivolous things and start a savings jar. We all have wants, and when we feel them in the moment, it sucks when we can't fulfill them. It sucks even more when you TRY anyways and it doesn't happen. It all boils down to how we choose to go about acquiring the desire. If the intention is already in the right place, then all that needs to be done is finding a new perspective to execute said intention!

One thing's for sure, it's A LOT easier said than done. I'm not here to tell you the transformation into your best self will be a Saturday morning stroll through the park. There are going to be times that this will take constant concentration, effort, and innovation to achieve your results, whether they be physical, mental, or spiritual (or most likely all three, but this depends on what you are trying to accomplish).

How To Beat Insanity 101

Before diving in, I'd like to clarify that when I talk about insanity, it isn't the medical definition. I've only gone over my personal description based on a quote. Understand that if you feel like you're in a state of psychosis or experiencing a chemical imbalance mentally, don't be afraid to seek help from others. You aren't weak at all. I applaud you for accepting your current circumstance because that takes true strength. A lot of people choose to mask their instabilities, and it only worsens their circumstances. So again, I'd be super proud of you for getting the help necessary.

Pertaining to the definition by NOT Albert Einstein, the methods to beat insanity are just like growing from any past behaviors; recognize the behavior that needs improving, self-reflect on all the factors that enable or influence it, list how you experience them, use what you've found out about yourself to find a common denominator in your experiences, and then use that as the foundation or improvement.

In my experience, I learned that one way I practice insanity was never admitting I actually had a problem. From checking my ex's social media to see if she talks about me, to feeling like being high wasn't enjoyable without adding Grabba Leaf to my weed, I was CONVINCED that I didn't have a problem. I was

Chapter Three

CONVINCED that I fully healed and was completely over this girl, yet I found myself clicking her profile multiple times a day. I was CONVINCED the amount I frequently smoked tobacco had no effect on my singing capabilities, yet I experienced more difficulty and injury than improvements. I was in complete denial, and no amount of peers or advice could have ripped me out of my self-sabotaging because I simply did not want the help! I didn't want the help because I just didn't know I needed it!

This is why I want to stress how important it is for YOU to recognize what YOU need to change. As much as I tried to heal from my past relationship, or as much as I wanted to sing like John Legend, I was stuck in a limbo-like state where my goals and my actions weren't aligning with each other. It was up to me and me ONLY to snap myself out of it and realize how severely I needed help. As much as I wish somebody else waved a wand and release me from the patterns I experienced, I was the one holding it.

I can not only imagine, but I'm confident that the same applies to you. Once you're willing to get yourself to this point (and I'm guessing you did since you're reading these words now), the next big step is figuring out how you personally practice insanity. For some, it could be prioritizing video games, overstudying, finding comfort in stagnancy, remaining a victim to a controlling parent/partner, or even something like constantly burning their hand on the stove to see if the flames hot. All of these things can feel normal to you only if you've already convinced yourself that enabling such behavior is for your greatest good. It's not only until after you find yourself out of it that you look back, feeling embarrassed that you could've ever let such things get in your way! Kind of like you'd get embarrassed when your parents show your partner your baby photos; it was once your reality! You've just grown so much from that past version of you that it's almost humiliating even remembering that was once where you were.

The good news is you always have the choice of staying in this stagnant timeline or growing into a new one that resonates more with the results you want. The bad news is it'll be much more challenging to commit to this growth than it will be to give up hope for the better. This process requires you to not only be harshly honest with yourself, but to wholeheartedly commit to unlearning and reteaching the values you have—very similar to the process of building/breaking a habit.

Forty-two days! That's the best estimate of how long it takes to not only break a bad habit but to also build a healthier one on top of it (twenty-one days for each one). If you were to only break a habit of insanity, especially one practiced for quite some time, chances are that you'll have a more difficult time staying away from relapsing shortly after, but more on that next chapter. For right now, don't worry about how long it will be until you achieve real recognizable results; let's just focus on starting the process and remaining committed to it.

One key factor in overcoming this is consistent intentional critiquing. Think about an aspiring professional basketball player trying to perfect his form. They have to do tedious things like stand in front of the hoop for HOURS, shooting the ball in the same exact way to rewire their muscle memory into shooting with more efficiency. From the position of their feet, knees, waist, shoulders, elbows, hands, and ball, to how high they need to jump, all of these things are calculated, executed, readjusted, and then repeated. The slightest slip up in their resolve can potentially erase all the progress made while undergoing their transformation, leaving them back at square one with the broken jumper they started with. That's actually a big reason why I really admire professional athletes and their stories of reaching greatness! The amount of dedication they need to not only perfect their craft, but also the faith required for their vision has been my reassurance that there is a light at the end of the tunnel, even when I'm consumed by the process and can't pick my head up to see it.

    Let's practice finding and focusing on your own vision. During your daily meditation (and I do hope it's become a daily practice now), bring your attention to the space in the middle of your forehead. The chakra that resides here is called your Third-Eye or Mind's Eye. This is the source for our ability to visualize the bigger picture and the necessary route to take to get there. When you practice insanity, your third-eye is probably clouded, which can be a leading cause of your unhealthy tunnel vision. Try listening to some third-eye guided meditations or some nature sounds to help get you out of your head (I personally find that sounds of the ocean or birds help the most). Take this time to go through all the different routes to your goal and simulate them, kind of like Doctor Strange in *Avengers: Infinity War*. You'll be surprised at how simple the most successful path was once you allow yourself to SEE IT.

 Once you see your desired route, it's essential that you truly commit to it. It's no use if you see the light but don't take any steps towards it. Remember to be willing to change. Get a calendar and set twenty-one-day markers you can build up to track your progress and encourage yourself to keep going. Once you get in the groove of implementing both the new perspectives with the habit-building/

breaking technique and I promise you'll find a way out just like I did.

Recap: If what you're doing isn't effectively getting you where you want to be, think of another path! Don't limit yourself because the tactic you're using is all you know. There are fifty ways to make a record, so be open to learning new ways to get your desired results and don't beat yourself up during the process. It's almost like a game of plug and chug; you won't really know if it'll work until you try it out yourself. A very tedious method, but after multiple failed attempts, you'll find that perfect form that Steph Curry can't even compete with (though I wouldn't put my money on it). So be kind, be patient, be open to growth, and stay committed to your bigger picture! Not on an individual path to get there.

Journaling Topic Question: What is the root of my cycles? How can I address it from the source?

Chapter Five

ADDICTION

"The priority of any addict is to anesthetize the pain of living to ease the passage of day with some purchased relief." - Russel Brand

Hi! My name is Brandon, and for quite some time, 'I've been an addict.

Now I'm not talking about snorting coke lines, or rolling MDMA at raves, or smoking crack on the street. I'm what you'd call a regular pot smoker and occasional psychedelic enthusiast. The reason I'm sharing this is not for you to tell me I should stop or that I'm ruining my life; 'cause, well, quite honestly, you were not with me shooting in the gym. In the simplest terms, those are my vices in this life. Like the purpose of me initially writing this book, I'm admitting the humanity of my situation to further understand who I am and sharing this self-reflection with you in hopes that it helps you on your journey to true happiness.

Also, I'd like to clarify that going forward, I'll be referring to drugs/addiction as any outside source of temporary satisfaction; narcotics, video games, junk food, you know, all the good stuff in life. Initially, drugs are fun! But anyone who's seen a drug abuse commercial or even saw a character in their favorite TV show start using knows that the fun phase isn't as long as people want it to be. If anything, the "fun" phase is extended if the person decides to put more effort into chasing that first high, which requires neglecting responsibilities, loved ones, and maybe even their own health.

If these things were used with moderation and self-control, people could make new friends who share common interests, find new hobbies they don't normally do, maybe even go to events they wouldn't have imagined enjoying, and that's the beauty of the "fun" phase! That step, whether it be drug-induced or not, will always bring more paths to indulge in. The only bad thing about it is, what happens when the intentions of wanting these experiences aren't pure?

Chapter Five

    It's like running away from your personal issues by meeting up with bad company can turn into accepting invites to people's parties you don't even know. Which can then turn into getting shit-faced with no one really there to make sure you get home safe. Addictions without awareness can lead you down some dangerous roads. Some people will reach this point in their life and realize that this isn't in their best interest (and I hope if you relate to this, you have the strength to know that you deserve to treat yourself better because true power lies in the ability to control your vices). However, unfortunately, there will still be people that don't see how damaging this can be to them. They're actively choosing to be blind to self-sabotage, and they won't realize it until they reach rock bottom and the Universe forces them to make a change. And even then, it's still up to them to choose if they want better for themselves or continue outdated patterns.

    Now, like I said before, drug use in its "usual" form is similar to things I've listed before, but let's not ignore the things that can be categorized as a drug that have less immediate/detrimental effects to the user. First, let's define what a drug is. A drug (thanks to a quick Google search) is a medicine or other substance that has a psychological effect when ingested or otherwise introduced to the body. With this guideline to follow, couldn't you place excessive eating, binge playing video games, or toxic sex under the category of drug use? (I might be high but stay with me here).

Don't get me wrong! I used to be the dude that got Chick-fil-a every day, and the kid who would stay up all night before school playing *Call of Duty*, and the little horn ball trying to fuck all my Twitter crushes during my late teens, and the man that rolled up hot spliffs before/during/after every single moment of life. During each of those times in my life, I didn't see anything wrong with it because it brought me happiness. It wasn't like I was inflicting self-harm or sulking in depression, or at least I didn't see it at first. What brought it to my attention (how these things became more of a drug instead of an enjoyable past time) was the same realization for all three situations. I found myself wrapped up in one small aspect of life, so much so that I sacrificed so many other things in life.

For food, it was money. Video games, it was goals. Sex, it was my friends. Spliffs, it was my health. In each respected situation, I came to the point where, since I was now aware (and acknowledged my self-sabotaging way of prioritizing lesser values over more important ones), it was truly up to me on whether or not I wanted better for myself or I wanted to accept the hole I dug.

That's when I made the connection in my head that a "drug" will be romanticized to a user until the end of days (or at least for me). It's almost as if it's how the human brain is programmed to help process certain things in life (or that can just be me going down another rabbit hole), especially if we've gone through something dramatic. We gravitate towards the specific things that bring our soul a sense of ease and comfort, whether that be narcotics, food, a lover, friends, pets, a thrilling experience, and all of that's okay! It's okay because we're all human, and having urges and tendencies like this is only a part of the choices that come with the journey. We have the choice to sidetrack, the choice to refrain from personal joy for the greater good of a goal, and (best of all) the choice to find a balance between the two.

I'll say it again and again, balance! You have to keep the oil on your spoon while experiencing what's outside of your task! As much as I'd absolutely love to fully indulge in my own addictions, I made a commitment to myself (and my Higher Self) that I wouldn't let my temporary desires distract me from accomplishing everything I set my eyes on. Abiding by this truly helped me write this book, complete my album, create my brand, and formulate a more descriptive blueprint for my future plans. The progress I made has been well worth the sacrifice! But what I didn't realize was that by completely removing myself from my worldly desires, I started becoming a workaholic machine. I became so absorbed in finding happiness in completing my goals that I neglected my present moment happiness.

Chapter Five

If it wasn't related to progress, forget it! I stopped smoking Grabba Leaf with my weed, which led to me heavily cutting back on smoking entirely. I stopped turning the TV on to avoid binging shows and only watched things that I knew for sure would inspire what I was working on. I stopped hanging out with people I considered close to me because I felt like time was of the essence and I couldn't afford to be wrapped up in other people's daily distractions. I became so dedicated to cutting out what felt unhealthy for my growth that it actually became unhealthy. I became addicted to "keeping my oil on the spoon."

I found myself switching from writing, singing, reading, graphic designing, songwriting, plotting, and starting the cycle over again. Whatever I could've done to keep my mind off of my past troubles while also being productive in whatever avenue I saw my future self in, I blindly dived headfirst. I began to antagonize any part of my personality that didn't resonate with what I was building. I guess you can say that in the end, I realized I was the antagonist in my own story.

I had to get it through my head that I'm only twenty-five! I'm young with the mindset that I'm 4,000,000,000 years old with seconds left to live. I have so much life ahead of me, and I've been beating myself up. I am constantly overthinking a day off when people my age don't even know what they want to pursue yet. Just like I don't need to chain smoke, binge play video games, habitually hang out with others, I don't need to overindulge in my life's work. In fact, doing so goes against everything I stand for.

Have you ever seen Pixar's *Soul*? Two beautiful things I'd like to reference are the lost souls and a soul's purpose. One character described the lost souls as "people that can't let go of their anxieties and obsession, leaving them lost and disconnected from life." Those big blobs repeating things like "make a trade" are the PERFECT examples for my point here. We can get so wrapped up looking for ways to make life better than what it currently is that we check out of the present moment. But actually, the trick is understanding that we are forever in the present moment!

Like the one that just passed as I'm typing this, the past moments are only a memory at this point. The future is only a present moment we have yet to experience. Now the butterfly effect is a very real lesson of wisdom, so being conscious of what you do right now and considering how that can lead to the desired future is essential, especially in my life. However, this great strength can quickly turn into your biggest weakness if you're so wrapped up in it that you become miserably obsessed in this moment. That tunnel vision can make you blind to the things right in front of you, and you just might miss the opportunity you were waiting for because you refused to open your eyes and see that it's in front of you.

Which leads to a soul's purpose (one more rabbit hole). We all have passions! Some people are skilled in specific activities, while others aren't. Some are extroverted, some are introverted, and others are somewhere in between. Some people feel that their purpose is to help others, and some believe that they need to destroy others. Does that make a particular soul's purpose more important than another? The answer is absolutely not. The truth I found is that no matter what anyone THINKS their purpose is, we were all sent to this Earth with one goal—to experience life.

No matter how you look at it, the things we tend to gravitate towards are the very things that make us feel alive. Everybody is attracted to something different, so it would only make sense that everyone finds their own reason to live in whatever sparks their inspiration. That's why I stopped judging people for how they choose to live or what hobbies they have, or even what vices they indulge in. Who are we to judge others when we go through the same things, just from a different perspective? Just like I've become addicted to becoming the best version of myself, to truly feel joy in every second I'm here, the same principle can be applied to somebody addicted to crack, or an athlete, or an inventor, or someone with hostile intentions to destroy the world we know. We're all just doing things that fuel the fire inside of us.

    It was this realization that helped me be more empathetic with not only others but also myself. There was no need to bash myself for doing things I enjoy, even if my hyper-active anxiety didn't deem it as productive. I didn't come back here to be this emotionless machine spitting out words that I didn't embody. I came here to indulge in all the abundance this life has to offer, which definitely includes sex, weed, video games, traveling, food, the career path I'm on, and so much more that I haven't experienced yet. We're all here for the experience. So, please don't get wrapped up in a tiny aspect of life and convince yourself that's the only way to find happiness. Learning your perfect balance of staying away from distractions to advance forward and allowing some lenience to just enjoy being alive is the lesson here. Learn from Icarus.

Addicts Anonymous

Alright, class! Settle down and take your seats. We'll start today's lesson by introducing ourselves and why we're here. Please flip to a blank page in your notebooks and write the following: "(Insert greeting of your choice)! My name is (insert name of choice here), and I'm an Addict! For (insert time period), I've (insert addiction) and have sacrificed (insert the cost of addition) because of it. It happened because I did not hold myself accountable for my actions. That changes now."

Look, I'm not here to tell you how to live your life for the same reasons you can't tell me how to live mine. YoU cAn'T teLL mE wHaT tO dO. Whether it's video games, sex, weed, partying, WHATEVER it may be. Find comfort in accepting your vice. Find comfort in knowing you're just as human as everyone else. There's no need to beat yourself up, especially since you're here now. You'll become strong enough to control your addiction once you can fully identify with it.

What this means is that you not only need to be aware of your addiction in order to conquer it, but you also need to understand why it is you're addicted to it. This matter usually stems from deep within the psyche where our nature of coping with trauma resides. So, don't be afraid to get some assistance to help unpack your thoughts and reach an understanding.

Therapy is something I not only encourage, but I also participate in as much as I can. I know my addictions and where they stem from, and I've reached a place where I can maintain a balance of "work hard, play hard." Yet, I still see my therapist periodically to check in and make sure I'm still practicing what we've discussed because I know how easy it is for me to convince myself that I "deserve" to overindulge. Even if it's for a reward, it bubbles down to the fact that I like to celebrate every accomplishment, so I'd end up overindulging more than I'd really want to. I've just found power in maintaining control over my desires.

Try this; when you're able to identify your addiction, think about why you're doing it WHILE doing it. Is it worth your time, energy, or health? Is it worth risking something you have, someone you care about, or your overall future? If it isn't worth your time and not worth the risk, then go read the last chapter over again before I throw a brick through this page. If the risk outweighs the worth, I shouldn't have to tell you that it's not a smart gamble. Now, if the worth outweighs the risks, then you should do what's in your power to keep your risks at a minimum. Kind of like how race cars get tune-ups during races or athletes stretch before a game. We'll call this process our scheduled maintenance.

Remember the make-or-break habit method? Well, during our maintenance, we'll apply this. For twenty-one days, I want you to completely stop indulging in whatever it is you're addicted to. COLD TURKEY. I can almost guarantee that those three weeks will be the longest, most dragged-out period you've ever been through, especially if your addiction has become a part of who you are. Just remember that it isn't forever; it's all test to see where you stand in both your addiction and resolve to control it. By the end of it, you'll have the freedom to indulge once more, but only if you choose to do so. If you've noticed yourself doing better off without it, then honor that. This method is to help show you the amount of power you have over it.

This battle is difficult, and it can be pretty easy to find a new addiction to cope with removing old ones if you're not aware of the root it stems from. The best advice I can give you is to practice patience, mediation, and optimism. Drink water or tea if you're craving a substance, exercise, or go on a walk if you're thinking about turning your TV on. Go spend time with your family that you're comfortable being around if you start getting consumed by temptation. Speak to your therapist if things get overwhelming and you lose sight of the light at the end of the tunnel. Use this time to build healthy habits as your foundations, so when the maintenance is complete, you can accurately assess the true benefit of indulging in the addiction again.

After that, it's all a matter of remembering to do this periodically to ensure that the awareness and control are solidified. The last thing we'd want is for you to go through the longest three weeks of your life and believe that the work stops there. The initial clean-up is always the worst. Keeping it clean after that is easy enough as long as you don't let the checklist go unchecked.

Recap: Don't ever give up! If you want to leave something in the past, do it! Anything outdated should not be picked up again. Remember that every step forward is the right step taken. Just keep swimming! You'll do fine.

Journaling Topic Question: What habits/people/things do I choose to believe I can't live without? How and why did this reliance start?

DIET

"Let food be thy medicine, and medicine be thy food." - Hippocrates

So, this? This shit right here? This, funny enough, is the meat and potatoes of the entire book. Is everyone familiar with the term "recipe to life?" In the culinary world, a recipe is a list of ingredients and instructions that should be followed to create a specific dish. Good thing for both of us, I'm in no way a master chef (although I can whip up a lovely meal out of the dozen dishes I know how to prepare). I'm just a poet who enjoys using common knowledge as metaphors of advice.

For my metaphorical meaning, a recipe, in the simplest terms, is a mapped-out path to the desired success. Want six packs abs? Go to the gym consistently! Want straight A's? You better study your ass off in every subject! The good thing is everybody's recipe isn't the same since everyone has their own unique individual goals. The bad thing is everybody's recipe isn't the same since everyone has their own unique individual goals. What works for them isn't guaranteed to work for you. But if your desired goal aligns with someone else, that doesn't mean you should just ignore their recipe. In fact, that gives you more of a reason to take note of what steps they've taken to reach their success.

Take Kobe Bryant, for example. Before becoming the phenomenal athlete we all admire, he watched Michael Jordan dominate in professional basketball, which was the same goal he was striving towards. Instead of flat out turning a blind eye and creating his own recipe for success, he acknowledged the greatness in Jordan's abilities. He took the time to not only study the way Jordan played, but he implemented it into his own practice. Any basketball fan can tell you how similar their styles are. And looking at it from this perspective, it only makes sense that following similar recipes achieve similar results.

Now, I already feel some of my lovely hard-headed readers thinking they don't need to follow

Chapter Six

anybody's recipe but their own, and my answer to them is that they are correct! No one else's recipe will ever be a sure-fire way to achieve your own unique, desired result. Worst case scenario, you can be allergic to their recipe (I can only imagine how corny that sounds) and end up poisoning whatever progress you've made.

The point of studying someone else's recipe is to not only pick out the things you like, but what also works best for your specific "dish." If what you want is vanilla cake, but you're allergic to eggs, their recipe containing them could possibly cause you harm in the long run. Yes, you'll have your cake, but what fun is it if you can't eat it too? (See what I did there?)

This in no way, shape, or form means that you can't have cake; it just means you can't have *their* cake. In the literal sense, vegans have used their creativity to come up with different ways to substitute animal products, and their end result was even more satisfying than baking something they couldn't enjoy too. The point I'm rambling about is; never discredit someone else's success, especially if they are in the same field you're in. Allow yourself to be open to new perspectives and algorithms that can get you the desired results in mind, but know yourself enough to distinguish what added tactics will be beneficial and what can be potentially harmful.

Until a year ago, you could say that I had the standard American diet; fried food, chicken/red meat every day, all the processed deliciousness you can think of! And If I'm honest, I went about six months straight where I would eat a meal from Chick-fil-a AT LEAST once a day. There was nothing in this world that I enjoyed more than their spicy deluxe sandwich with sweet and spicy sriracha sauce for the fries. NOTHING. It wasn't until I had an epiphany (during one of my psychedelic trips) that I realized how vital not only food, but my entire diet, was to my "recipe."

To give you some insight (and provide some brief entertainment), I've had some pretty out-of-the-box experiences with all my psychedelic trips. From the feeling/visualizing of how all things are connected, to being reintroduced to the trauma I didn't know I was still healing from, to even understanding what I liked versus what I thought I liked because others liked it; each individual experience provided a mind-opening perspective that I wasn't aware of before. One common factor through all of them was that I realized that my body and mental state were susceptible to whatever I indulged in, let alone paid attention to. For starters, I couldn't eat anything other than fruits because everything else tasted like blended cardboard, or I would overthink about the animal I was chewing on and instantly spit it out. Trust me, this was a VERY confusing and disturbing, yet enlightening time in my life.

    Now (me being the curious, self-aware person I am), I took it one step further and observed how I reacted to certain things, like certain tv shows, cell phones, other people, their aura, and how it affected me. I used each of my psychedelic experiences to further understand who I am and what/who it is I truly find comfort in. Being in such an emotionally vulnerable state helped bring my attention to what makes me feel good and the things that bring me down. Above all that, my biggest epiphany came to me after analyzing all of my observations. If certain things boosted or diminished my state of being during my psychedelic trips, do those things have the same influence on me even when I'm not in an altered state?

I'm proud to say that I took that extra step, and since December 21st, 2019, I haven't eaten any land animals. Not only that, but I was also recently able to take it one step further and became a part of the vegan community (it took almost a year to get to that point, though). Now as much as I love how I feel with my new diet, I'm not going to be one of those Jehovah's Witness-like vegans and tell you this is the right way to live, and if you don't convert, then you're doomed to never achieve what you want. You see, changing my diet, although it was a significant change, was merely the first stepping stone in testing my self-discipline. I needed to test that I was not only aware of what works and doesn't work for me, but that I could commit to wanting better for myself and had self-restraint against things that aren't necessarily harmful but don't align with my highest timeline.

Before I changed my life through this intention (and set an excellent example for you to follow), I needed proof that my hypothesis could be supported by my own experiments and not just "he said, she said." The hypothesis being: if I practice discipline in a major aspect of my life (like what food I nourish my body with), then I can use that success as motivation to expand that discipline in other areas of my life. At the very least, I can say it would've been A LOT easier to write these words and tell you to follow them rather than sticking to them myself. But I needed to lead by example. If you're someone who struggles with self-sabotaging tendencies, this topic will probably be the most difficult to implement into your life thus far, but that's only confirmation that you have the potential to reap the most benefits in the long run. It's time for growth!

Maintaining A Balanced Diet

To make this easier to digest, *queue rimshot* let's look at it as a food diet. First, we'll have to list EVERYTHING that can be a part of your diet. Make sure not to leave anything out! It's crucial that you have a visual in front of you that shows the extent of what you "eat" so, in the long run, you have an idea of all the things you were once indulged in. Good, bad, ugly, embarrassing; write it out! Intentionally leaving the smallest of things out can unknowingly sabotage your progress (or at the very least be very triggering; please just take my word on this one rather than finding out for yourself).

Perfect! Now that you can see what your current diet consists of, the next step is figuring out what goal you're striving for. If it's to simply be a more "you" version of yourself, then circle the components of your diet that resonate with how you define yourself. These are the things that you need to put your attention into. See anything on your list that doesn't resonate with you? That's okay! Just cross them out and keep in mind that this is something you'll start avoiding. So, if your goal is to lose weight and you habitually eat a five-course midnight snack, maybe that's something you'll have to stop. As much as I wish it wasn't true, sacrificing some of the things that make us happy can be the catalyst for us to transform into our happiest selves. Are you rolling your eyes? It's okay, I am too.

Once you're able to establish your current diet's pros and cons, it's time to build on top of that foundation with new components that further resonate with your goal. If you've gotten control over your late-night munchies and stuck to your daily smoothies, it's now time to hit the gym! Study what someone in your desired position should already be knowledgeable about and apply it! You'll be surprised at what it REALLY takes to be in the position you want to be in. As dull or intimidating or drawn out as it may be, their diet worked. Just like at one point we all complained about having to eat our vegetables and take our vitamins, I bet a lot of us are thankful we did, looking back on it at least.

When it comes to handling things on your list that aren't as easy as crossing a line through it, my best advice (without knowing anything about you and your personal experience) would be to remove yourself from any potential connections to whatever it is. If you want to stop your social media addiction to focus more, delete the apps entirely. If your toxic, controlling family is restricting you from spreading your wings, then you HAVE to remove yourself from their nest. When reinventing your mental diet, it's necessary to stay away from any potential triggers. Although you still need to be disciplined enough to make sure you don't "relapse," it's best to keep them out of sight entirely. Trust me, I speak from experience.

    Do what you need to do in order to stick to your diet! Think of it as the only thing in between you and your dream-self, because truthfully, it is. Just like you won't see your acne magically vanish overnight, the results will show little by little as you stay consistent. Don't beat yourself up for not seeing immediate changes. Don't give up and revert to old ways because you had a slip-up. The key is to have faith in the process! The recipe you've created is how you'll get that masterpiece you crave. As long as you remain open to constantly adding beneficial ingredients, your diet will pave your very own Paradise Parkway.

Recap: Be aware of what it is you eat, drink, watch, all of it! Find your own recipe for success and stick to it!

Journaling Topic Question: What does my food palette look like when I'm at my most physically embodied? How can I be more present and intentional with my meals?

COMPANY

"You are the average of the five people you spend the most time with." - Jim Rohn

Take a second to think about the people closest to you. Can you notice any similar mannerisms you guys share? From lingo and body gestures, to fashion style, consider EVERY way we as humans express our individualism (although it probably feels less individualistic now that I think about it). It's very common to share the same taste of music or food with someone you're close with, but why is that?

Naturally, it's human nature to gravitate towards people or places that help us feel like we belong. Remember your first day of high school? It was probably easy to feel like the social pariah (or at least it was for me). But as time passed, you'd meet someone by talking about your favorite show or wearing those exclusive shoes that just released, and you guys realize how much you have in common after talking. Sooner than you even realize, you find yourself going to different gatherings on the weekends with your very own new clique! Now, this is something wonderful to experience, and I hope you have been able to feel the pure joy of having a group of people you can relate to and enjoy spending time with, but how long does that last?

That sounds like such a negative question. I apologize! I really don't mean to seem like a pessimist when I say this, but how many can say they are still as close to their high school/college friends as they were before? For those of you who can prove me wrong, the reason the friendship lasted is most likely because you guys continuously shared common mindsets and goals while both individually striving in your own lane. And that right there is one of the most unique types of connections one can experience in this life. The only thing is a lot of us don't end up finding soul-mate-like friendships so early in life, for the simple fact that we aren't so sure who we even are just yet.

See, it's very typical for an adolescent to find out more about themselves by exploiting their interests with their friends. I feel as if this stage of life is where teens discover more about how to express/indulge their soul desires, such as hobbies, sexuality, long-term goals, etc. In my own experience, this was the time in which I saw everyone changing from doing all the basic kid interests to finding fun in going out to drink, smoke, and hook up. Anything that helped us feel more like the grown-up version of ourselves we wanted to be. What a time to be alive! If I could rewind my life and live those very memorable nights again, I would. ONLY if the blast from the past lasted no longer than the exact moment of enjoyment. Don't get me wrong, I'm grateful for my entire high school experience (especially senior year), but I can say very confidently that both the moments and the people in those moments are in my past where they belong.

The sad fact is we can't crystalize those moments of joy and apply them to the present time we're in. Trying to do so only leaves you with your hands filled with shattered hopes and dreams. Everything in this life is in a constant state of change. Everything is in a continuous state of evolution. So how you handle a situation today will be entirely different to how you handled it years ago because that time gave you the experience and wisdom needed to apply what wasn't accessible before.

So, what do you do when you evolve and no longer identify with the group? Well, you can either do the healthy thing and immediately stop spending so much time with them, or you can let that stagnant energy fester and manifest into the self-sabotage hindering your growth like I did!

This is a lesson that I, unfortunately, had to experience first-hand; otherwise, I would be stuck in the constant loop for all of eternity. It was my overly loving nature and empathetic heart that stopped me from setting boundaries with people I've been close to for years, and that only led to my own downfall (oh, you want to know the tea now, huh?). To give you some insight, I ran away from my family problems for an extended period of my life by finding comfort in other people. I thought that since my blood-related family didn't seem to understand (let alone WANT to understand) me, I could fill that void by building my own family with my group of friends. This led to me becoming a constant giver to my friends, which made me feel like I was their parent. Providing them with rides if they didn't have a car, a place to hang out and feel safe physically and mentally, and an ear willing to listen and help them through whatever problem life threw at them. Don't get me wrong, I love these people (I still do) and absolutely love being able to be a positive influence in their life. Yet, after years passed and my void from childhood wasn't healing, it became apparent to me the situation I unconsciously put myself in.

The love I gave out was barely ever reciprocated how I needed it, and I always found myself dealing with issues feeling alone, which shouldn't have been the case. If I constantly surrounded myself with people to avoid feeling alone, why was it still something I couldn't avoid? I started to realize how one-sided some of these connections were, and I decided to really ask myself why I had them in my life in the first place.

What it bubbled down to was something that some of you are probably familiar with, too; each connection was its own form of a trauma bond. For those of you who aren't familiar with the term, a trauma bond is when an abused person finds emotional attachment to their abuser or someone who demonstrates similar traits of their abuser. After learning this and putting it into perspective, I realized my group of friends and how they lived their life was identical to the issues I was initially trying to run away from. The same feelings of manipulation, misunderstanding, and lack of empathy were present. I only overlooked it because I wanted them to be my safe place away from the manipulation, misunderstanding, and lack of empathy I was already feeling at home; it sounds like insanity, doesn't it?

    Remember the quote at the beginning of this chapter? Well, from looking at the closest people of my life at that time, I'm the average of substance abuse, toxic masculinity, narcissism, entitlement, and determination. Would you want to be my friend?

    Of course, not! And at that point, neither would I. For quite some time, I beat myself up for putting myself in such a situation and not being aware of how it affected me for so long. Even with my new understanding, I still found optimism and room in my heart to attempt to help my loved ones improve their lives instead of enabling their unhealthy habits, which evidently failed terribly. So terribly that the Universe forcibly purged everyone out of my life in the span of seven days, and I was left with nothing but peeled off Band-Aids and new trauma to heal from.

But the good news is this is in the past! I might still be healing, but that's a lifetime journey. I will say that each day gets more manageable for me to find peace because of the daily progress I make for myself. These days, the people I keep close to me make me the average of maturity, stability, financial literacy, love, and self-sufficiency. All things that I either want for myself or already see within me.

Again, it wasn't until I got to this point that I realized how much the people I keep around affect me, so if you're experiencing the same thing, remember to stay kind to yourself. Cutting out people you hold close to your heart is truly one of the most painful things emotionally, especially if you're like me and don't have it in you to be heartless to them. But trust the process! Remember, this journey is about becoming the best you, and whoever is meant to be on it with you will be there through thick and thin. So take a deep breath, visualize your best self, and trust your process of transformation. Your soul tribe is waiting just outside of this growth.

Company Awareness for Dummies

It's human nature to want to be accepted by the collective. In theory, we have the option to gravitate towards groups that are either familiar (in the sense of family, long-lasting friends, or a situation that seems similar to what you're used to) or something completely new. The best advice I can share on this is to follow what feels right and what helps you grow simultaneously. Stagnancy means it's time for a change, and right when you clear up that space is when the Universe will replace it with something even better than what you asked for. Have faith in yourself and your individual path!

Kind of like how you have to pay attention to the ingredients in your "diet," you should be aware of the people that are a part of your recipe. As much as we'd like to think of our loved ones as the kind, supportive, compassionate people we see them as, there can very well be a rotten egg in the bunch. If we could literally crack their shell like a real egg, then it'd be easier to differentiate the rotten from the good! Unfortunately, that's not the ethical or legal way to go about things, so let's just keep this metaphorical, please (I am not liable or responsible for anyone who takes my metaphors in the literal sense).

In order to make this omelet, the shells we'll have to crack are going to take some psychological background. Reading the previous chapters and keeping a journal to maintain self-awareness can even be the preparation needed to understand how other people are. The better you get at picking up on the little things, the better you'll be at differentiating who you should/shouldn't be around.

Chapter Seven

  Have you ever been excited about something huge happening in your life and wanted to tell your friend, but when you did, they somehow made a joke about it? Or maybe they projected their own fears of failure on you? Or perhaps they were completely dismissive to what was obviously bringing you a sense of happiness? These are all examples of company you shouldn't be around. When you're happy about something, your company should amplify that feeling, not tear it down. What that means is you're surrounded by people that either don't see your vision, don't honestly care for you, don't believe in themselves, or they're so wrapped up in their own life it's become their own psychosis. Either way, dump their ass! If holding their hand brings you down, then you're going to have to let them go eventually. If not, those connections will be forced out, and trust me, it's never fun.

  The company you should keep around are people that support and encourage you to pursue whatever it is that makes you happy. I'm not talking about yes-men. I'm talking about people that not only tell you they care but show you in the smallest of ways. I tend to notice someone's genuine empathy in ways like asking questions for further details, giving their undivided attention, and doing what's in their power to help the cause. But the little things are defined differently by anyone, just like we all have our own love languages.

You'll probably find that the people you want to gravitate to are the ones that know how to love you correctly, but can you define what that looks like? There's a reason why you should love yourself before loving another. Bonding with someone for the sake of avoiding loneliness is one of the most popular ways people get wrapped up in bad company. That's when people end up in situations that they don't feel resonates with them, which can be scary, dangerous, or just uncomfortable in general. Whatever the case is, it could've been avoided by honoring who they are.

All it could've taken was a simple, "Nah, I don't drink" or "you guys go ahead, I'm gonna call it a night." It doesn't seem so easy when that company guilt trips you, but you shouldn't have to put up with it anyways. Your loneliness is what put you in this predicament, and ironically, being alone is what will get you out.

I can't stress this enough! Love yourself! Know yourself! Figure out what you need from the people in your life and cut out the ones that don't fit that mold. Don't worry too much about finding a new company to replace the old one. Focus on what already works for you and cater to that. The Universe has a funny way of giving you just what you're looking for when you aren't looking for it, so keep that in mind. Make sure that when you do open yourself up to company again, you do it from a place where you can clearly see who's suitable for your omelet and who you should maintain boundaries with. That way, you don't need to worry about looking over your shoulder or being dragged down because the foundation starts from within you. All you must do to build on top of it is honor it. Sooner or later, you might just find yourself with a whole village backing your cause; just you wait!

Recap: Not all company is good company! Learn how to be happy on your own and the Universe will bring you the people that resonate with who you truly are. The main thing stopping that from happening is refusing to let go of the bad company you keep running back to. Be strong! Be disciplined! It's for a greater purpose.

Journaling Topic Question: Who in my life uplifts me? Fuels me? Who in my life drains me? Depletes me? What do these relationships say about what I'm emitting?

Chapter Eight

PATIENCE

"Drop by drop is the water pot filled." - Buddha

Inch by inch. Brick by brick. Day by day. All of these commonly used phrases get overlooked due to their simplicity. But this simple advice is actually the secret to life, which in my opinion is both equally fortunate and misfortunate. You see, it's one wonderful thing to know the secret ingredient for success because it's almost like having the cheat code to avoid any unnecessary headaches or frustrations. It's another thing when you realize the cheat is, well, there are no cheats. Like it or not, all things happen in their own time. There is no magical *Click* remote that can fast forward to the end of the journey. Your water pot will be full once it's filled with every droplet necessary, no matter how long it takes.

Now I'll be honest, as much as I tell myself "brick by brick" every day, I have trouble finding comfort in it. I thought understanding the need for patience would make it come to fruition, but that would've been too easy! Little did I know, obtaining this wisdom was only the first step. The next step was actually engraving this simple lesson into the deepest part of my subconscious, and this is a battle I STILL struggle with from time to time.

It's like a child finding out what they're getting for Christmas a whole year in advance. The secret's out! It's theirs to enjoy, but not until the years up. So, what do they do? I'm not sure how you would answer this, but my first guess would be that they'll put on a theatrical show about how they'll die from waiting so long, or maybe that tantrum turns into rage. Either way, the anticipation alone will drive them bonkers, and that's why they are the perfect example to describe my own personal impatience.

Knowing what my future holds influences my viewpoint of the time frame before that. In other words, I know my dreams and aspirations are rightfully mine because they resonate with everything I am and want to become. I know that everything is achievable, and there will be a time when I can bask in all the trophies of my accomplishments; it's just that I can be so fucking impatient. The fact that I know what I'm striving towards is already rightfully mine isn't enough to satisfy the endless anxiety I can feel at times and instead feeds the enraging flame. I can get so caught up in my current circumstances that I forget that it's not permanent. A perfect expression of this would be something I went through pretty recently.

(Imagine me jumping into a time portal to emphasize a flashback moment.)

As of today, I'll be moving across the country to California in 19 days. This is a decision I made back in late September, and since then, I've used my time to focus on preparing for this leap of faith. I am a combination of all the emotions imaginable when I think about it: a whole new state, a new ocean, new air quality, MOUNTAINS. The thought of the new experience fills me with so much passion it really brings me to tears.

Now, for a while, I was upset with myself for

setting a date more than three months away for me to start my life's next chapter. The plane ticket wasn't expensive, and my aunt and uncle were already willing to welcome me into their apartment. I already had nothing really fueling my drive, passion, and overall happiness here (my hometown, Pembroke Pines in Broward County, Florida). But the thought of leaving so soon after my life took a plummet made me feel like I would've been running away from my problems.

Just tucking that fresh trauma away deep in the darkest corner of my head and forgetting it ever happened. You know, fake it 'til you make it. But that's not the route I wanted to take. I understood my goals were on the other side of hell. If I ran to California so quickly, who knows who I would've become? The one thing I'm sure of was this; if I didn't heal in the place where I felt the pain, then it would always be there whenever I came back. And that's the last thing I wanted. Before I started my next life chapter, I had to be this book's living word. I couldn't let my problems simmer on the back burner when I was trying to empower the community to triumph over their obstacles.

(Imagine life fast-forwarding for a cinematic transition into a glimpse of the future.)

It's been about forty days since I wrote the words above. I just took four edible cookies to celebrate the small, yet monumental accomplishments made today. I woke up at my aunt's house in San Francisco, California, at 8 A.M. and got picked up by my uncle to go running six miles across the Pacific shoreline. I bonded with my extended family and got to hear stories about my parents and grandfather that I've never heard before. I created a YouTube channel for the company I started to be the umbrella for all of my creations, such as my vlogs, music/music videos, and other ventures, like this book. I've kept my head down and focused on so many productive ventures that it's become a joy to wake up every day and do it over again. I've found a perfect balance of being the man I am while also catering to my inner child. My proof is writing this at 11:30 P.M. while rewatching

Dragon Ball Super. All while these edibles are smacking the shit out of me.

    Why was I worried? In these three weeks that I've been in California, I've had more progress than I could've imagined. All of it is because I really put myself through the hell of dealing with all of my problems head-on, leaving me open for all the opportunities presented to me. I established my very own company with the LLC pending as I type. I have a more complete concept and track listing for my premiere album while incorporating ideas that sparked my inspiration to even make music.

    I have both the evidence, confidence, and wisdom to say that I know that waiting for the daily bricks to finally form into a house can and will feel like a never-ending time loop of the same day over and over again. But hey, here I am. I looked up and started seeing I've completed the house's framework. All that's left is to build my roof, the crown that will sit on top of the foundation. Sorry if I'm not making sense, the edibles kicked it up another notch just now... *completely zones out*

Chapter Eight

(Fast-forwarding to the next day.)

    I'm sitting here reading what I wrote high as shit, and it makes me giggle with both joy and confusion. That's what I chose to do with my time, and I considered it fun! Struggling to concentrate enough to articulate my thoughts to you has really become a form of therapeutic entertainment, and I love it. Just like my high ass was saying, my brick house is almost complete, and it's all because I allowed myself to be patient with the daily progress.

    Yesterday, I could have forced myself to finish this chapter (and at this current time, these last few pages of this chapter were the final pages I had to free write before I dived into the second half of each chapter you've been experiencing). Still, I chose to leave it in the hands of the me of tomorrow. I've learned to be content with whatever progress I make within a day's time because I know I put in my very best effort to keep moving forward in pursuing my goals. Every. Damn. Day. Another brick gets cemented in my dream home. Another flower blooms in my garden. Another droplet fills my bucket.

At this point, I honestly don't know another way to tell you guys the beauty of patience other than speaking from experience. Patience isn't an ability that someone just unlocks out of nowhere. It's the wisdom obtained by applying its lessons every single day, in every aspect of life.

In fact, as I'm proofreading this back, I'm pretty pleased with how everything came together. Especially this chapter. Instead of forcing myself to place every brick down in one sitting, I wrote on multiple occasions, and it evolved into a sneak peek of the next venture I'm exploring (that's if you catch on)—a detail that I probably could've gone without, yet adds even more of my personality into these pages. All because I chose to do today's work and left tomorrow's work for tomorrow.

Sooner than you know it, you'll be able to look up and see the foundation just like I have. Sooner than later, you'll be so inspired by all the things you persevered through to reach that point, and you'll look at yourself as your very own role model, both in patience and everything else this life has to offer. This I promise you, my dear friend.

Remember, it's all in divine timing. Always.

Practicing Patience For The Impatient

Take a deep breath. One that fills every cell in your body with life, imagine yourself as the planet itself and that your inhales are the very same winds that touch your skin. The bliss of stillness washes over any tension or uneasiness you feel as you surrender to the present. And at this very moment, the only things that matter are your breath and these words.

Now, if you're ever in a moment where this isn't the case, then that's okay. Put this down and pay attention to what the Universe is currently presenting you. As far as I know, this book isn't going to run off anywhere. It also wasn't written with the intention to finish within a time limit and *poof*; magically, all your problems are fixed. Even though I wanted to complete all my goals, including this book, as quickly as possible to relish in the trophies, I knew it wouldn't have made a difference if I completed them in seven days or seven months. I've come to the understanding that my destiny is already written in the stars. I'm merely in the middle of my story, and so are you. In that case, I saw no need to slave in front of the computer for unhealthy lengths of time to force my healing.

In the end, it honestly would've ended up being more counterproductive than not writing at all. I knew that it would all come together when it was time, so I was compelled to only write when I felt like I had both the free time and inspiration to do so. If forcing myself and intentionally letting myself write will lead to the same desired result, why would I put myself in harm's way and strain for it? The same applies to how you should go about not only this book, but all things in this life. Remember to stop and smell the flowers more than just occasionally. Like easter eggs in video games, you might find a hidden gem just like the one I put a few pages ago.

Are you getting tired of me blabbering about my experience with patience instead of getting to the point? Well, sorry to tell you, but all of it was a test. How you're feeling right now should tell you the amount of patience you already have. Congratulations to everyone who had no problem getting through it without shaking their leg or fidgeting; you passed the test!

If you have difficulty finding patience, then these journaling and meditation exercises have probably been challenging for you to stay consistent with, let alone fully take the initial step. However, there's a reason I bring them up, because I really believe that throughout my growth process, these things have been excellent tools that assisted me. Whenever I feel myself losing my patience, I immediately close my eyes, repeat my affirmations, and remind myself that everything happens for me, not TO me. This way, it's become a regular practice, and anything that challenges my stamina is only a training exercise to further embody my patience.

It takes time! Especially when you first start off, you'll feel out of your element or like you can't sit still long enough to really focus. That's where "brick by brick" comes into play for you. Initially, you must condition yourself to place down a brick that represents what patience is to you. Then you have to stay consistent in order to create your foundation around this. That's when you'll build on top of that and begin to see how much has changed from point zero to point, uh, now (you get the point *boom*). For now, we'll focus on the foundation.

Let's start with meditation. When I talk about meditating, I don't mean just closing your eyes and sitting there for five to ten minutes; the real magic is what's happening inside. The biggest obstacle you'll face is having to quiet your mind to tap into "the zone," as *Soul* would call it. The most effective method I've found is to sit in complete and utter silence and, in your head, count backward from 100 down to 0. Then repeat, starting from 80, then from 60, then 40, and lastly, 20. This isn't a race! Try to count as slow as you possibly can. You'll find that it can get rather challenging to silence the side chatter in your head to the point where you might even forget what number you were on, but focus! I've found that after completing my full count, my headspace is

Chapter Eight

completely cleared to the point that things that bothered me before no longer have an intense effect on me. That's the goal of obtaining patience, becoming unbothered by any outside force to deal with it in the proper, most efficient way.

Allow yourself to experiment! Although I'm preaching about meditation in the form of sitting crisscross apple sauce, there's plenty of different ways to tap in. Yoga, journaling, walks in the park, puzzles, playing sports, preparing and cooking food, reading (like you're doing right now), literally anything that requires your full attention and brings you bliss. Although conditioning your patience doesn't always involve things you currently enjoy, these are acceptable starts to figuring out what works best for you.

If you really want to challenge yourself and see some worthwhile results, then do the things that would frustrate you the most. For me, it was listening to my peers' gossip. As much as I love them, gossip is something I don't really have an interest in. It came to a point where my impatience led to me becoming dismissive of what they'd want to talk about, which led to them believing I didn't care about what they had to say. It made it difficult for me to initiate collaborations. But no! I just didn't care about what they were saying at the moment! I wanted to talk about making money and changing the world and aliens, ya know? The only problem was that I couldn't fast forward through the gossip to get to those conversations.

To reach that destination, I had to be fully present through the ENTIRE journey. I had to accept that this was a part of the process and I would have to sit through this stage, which is why I chose to challenge myself in this specific situation. Apply this to your own experiences! I didn't learn to like gossip because that shit is trash, and I personally think there are better ways to spend my time. I learned to accept that there are people who don't feel the same way as I do about it, and if it's something they care about, and I care about them or at the very least wanted to build with them, then I would have to become less dismissive.

Chapter Eight

Take your time. Be kind to your process, and treat your patience as a muscle. Exercise it frequently, push your limits, and it'll grow periodically. In time, you'll be able to see the house you've built with each brick. The result is one of the greatest feelings, definitely well worth it.

Recap: Breathe! Let the stars align on their own.

Journaling Topic Question: In what areas of my life can I intentionally slow down? Where does the belief that I need to rush stem from?

LOVE

"Love yourself first and everything will fall into line."
-Lucille Ball

BEFORE YOU START THIS CHAPTER, I WANT TO SAY PLEASE, don't laugh at me. Laugh with me. THIS RIGHT HERE? EMBARRASSING!!! HAHAHAHAHAHAHA, OKAY, ENJOY!

(Flashback to November 2nd, 2020)

Quick update. I'm currently writing this to you on the balcony looking over Downtown Miami and the water surrounding it. I'm smoking the finest weed money can buy and dressed up in a new outfit, feeling ready to start this next chapter in my life.

You see, behind me is a romantically decorated surprise for the girl I hold very close to my heart for her birthday. I covered the room with roses and petals and placed three wrapped gifts stacked on top of one another in a pyramid shape. I got her a new speaker, Jordans I knew she wanted, a Telfar bag I ordered for her (back when we were together), a new vinyl record player, and a vinyl to go with it. Now I should mention that this was not an ordinary vinyl. This specific vinyl was a 1 of 1 limited edition that'll never be made again (or at least an authentic copy) made by none other than the man typing these words right now. Yes. I made a unique project just for her, with a picture of her that I drew, for the cover.

So much effort, emotion, execution, energy, and time went into the initial fight I had with myself about whether I should be doing anything for her considering that we broke up. And then that transitioned into the realization that if I love her and want to make this work, I have to show her how committed I am to the relationship and the bigger picture. Then that followed with brainstorming the infinite ideas I had for her birthday, which (at the time) was a month away. After deciding to book a hotel room and give her the freedom to decide to come was the most effective way to communicate without turning it into an argument, I started planning.

Now, I'm just going to say this, it is not an easy task to accomplish such an intricate idea with the timeframe I had, especially with the little help I had at hand. I mean, I had ten days to write songs, record them, and create the front and back cover art for the vinyl sleeve for it to be printed, pressed, and shipped from Amsterdam in time to make it to Miami in twenty days. I completely stressed myself the fuck out trying to do the absolute most for somebody who stopped responding to me, but being able to see the finished product after all the hard work really made me happy. This process helped me not only create a very unique birthday gift, but it also helped me stay productive and allowed me to express what I was feeling through multiple forms; letting me genuinely become aware of everything I was going through.

For all of you that think I'm foolish to do this for someone I'm not with, let alone not responding to me, I would say you're absolutely correct! In my past, I've been a complete simp for whoever I was in love

Chapter Nine

with. I aim to give the woman I marry the most beautiful, thoughtful, passionate relationship ever experienced in all her lifetimes. But I don't really know who I'll end up with. That's the reason why when I love, I love HARD. There's no gray area for me. It's either "I love you, and I mean it when I say I got you," or "read x no reply." I'm not going to sit here and tell you that this mindset hasn't led to heartbreaks or painful experiences. I will say that after the fact, I'm always happy that I chose love instead of ang—

(Seven Weeks Later)

There's a reason I stopped there. Unfortunately, as I was in the hotel room putting the finishing touches together for the woman who wouldn't come in until I left, I received news that my grandma, who was fighting COVID-19, passed away. I was distraught, but somehow, I compartmentalized it so that I could finish preparing the room. At that point, I realized that I needed to give this gift more than my ex needed to receive it. I wanted to shower her with love because life is short and death is inevitable. Going so long without spending time with her interfered with my happiness; I couldn't imagine not having her there for me at a time like this. But that's precisely what happened.

Before I go on, I'd like to clarify that I am not perfect; the fact that I'm writing this book about my vulnerable experiences is proof enough. This woman was not evil. What you're getting is merely a tiny portion of a much larger story from only one person's perspective. As much as I wanted to see and talk to her, I've come to terms with the fact that I was getting this treatment because I actually broke her heart by not loving myself correctly.

Now, this doesn't excuse her for how she's treated me; the simple truth is I have no control over how things will play out, no matter how detailed the plan may be. I have control over the actions I take, yet no control over the outcome of it all at the same time. The only hope I have is to learn from the past, so when a similar situation comes about, I have a better understanding of what does and doesn't work. In this case, I had to dig deep, and I mean *DEEP* into my psyche, to understand the root of all the problems I've experienced.

What I found was, well, that I loved everybody! I always tried to make sure everyone around me was comfortable, and if they needed a favor, I never hesitated to lend a hand. I'd stop what I was doing if a friend needed a ride, changed my plans to work around others, even opened up my home to be the central headquarters where people could have a free space. I wanted to do all of these things, and even now, I still want to help people, but it's crucial to understand where that kindness is coming from and how I act on that kindness.

If you're anything like me, you already understand how being an over-giver is a double-edged sword, especially when gratitude isn't often shown. Because of my upbringing and personality (sprinkled with a heavy load of trauma I've suppressed), I saw someone else happy as a source of happiness. It got to a point where it became my primary distraction so that I didn't have to think about whatever issues I had going on, and that was the problem. What was supposed to be a pure expression of love and support to another turned into my escape from reality. I realized I would immediately look to perform an act of kindness the second my introspection took a dark turn, which unfortunately happened more hourly than daily.

Now, being under the impression that if I were to treat other people's issues as if they were more important than my own so I didn't worry about mine had its pros and cons. A benefit that came from it was that once I was done making everyone else happy, I then had new wisdom and inspiration to make myself happy! I could look at my problems from a different perspective where the size of the problem didn't intimidate me from taking that first step. If I'm having a similar issue as one that I helped someone else conquer, I could simply apply what I felt would assist me in my own experiences. Being the problem solver for others boosted my happiness, but being my own problem solver is what really sustained it.

The downfall for putting others before myself was honestly a lot more extensive than I first imagined it. You see, while helping others can feel like a very pure gesture, it can very quickly turn into one's own self-destruction. For me, I found myself running towards others and their issues to avoid truly doing the shadow work that I needed to do. I treated it like my drug, and I ended up putting myself in positions where I was over-giving help even when it wasn't appreciated or acknowledged. At this point, I was the epitome of insanity, going back and helping the same unappreciative people and hoping that the decaying joy would somehow return (kind of like chasing that first high). And when I got the results I didn't want but should've expected, I felt even more shitty inside. On top of having a mountain of unattended issues of my own, I began to feel defeated by intimidation when my go-to quick fix started to fail me. My dark thoughts would become unavoidable, coming back stronger than ever with new fuel to feed their fire so I can lose all the progress I've strived for. All because I didn't correctly love ME.

    I can happily say with confidence that I'm both proud of who I used to be as well as who I am now. That toxic kindness is what brought me the wisdom and peaceful solitude that I relish in today. The one thing I will say is that I'm very relieved that it's in the past. I don't blame anyone for treating me the way they did. I don't wish malice towards anyone. I don't want to see what karma has in store for them. I genuinely wish them the best because I realized that the root problem wasn't their reactions to my gestures but more so where the gestures were coming from. My lack of self-love and control over my emotions is what fueled my passion for helping others, no matter what I got in return.

Fighting Cupid

I know the quote is about loving yourself first, and I just confessed about how I've constantly put others before me, but I want us to learn what NOT to do for this lesson. Just like I'm doing, use this as wisdom to make sure you don't find yourself in a similar situation. Put yourself before any lover, friend, or family member... ALWAYS. As beautiful as it starts, love that turns unhealthy can be one of the biggest distractions on your life path. The biggest lesson I've learned through these experiences is how essential practicing detachment is when it comes to this.

    Detachment doesn't mean let it go; it means let it be. Understand that the only thing in this life you really have control over is yourself. You do not, cannot, and will not control anyone else. Love without exercising detachment can quickly become an obsession, just like it did for me. Whether it's a controlling parent, obsessive lover, or an extreme fanatic on the sidelines, unhealthy love can be the catalyst to why you lose what it is you love in the first place.

    At this point, I don't know how I can turn this around and make it into something uplifting and inspirational so that this chapter isn't depressing, and I think I'm okay with that. This is the chapter where I'm not trying to be strong for both of us; I'm letting myself be real and feel what I'm feeling. I've come to terms with the fact that as much as I want to have intimacy in my life, I'm still closed off after the turn of events that happened. I've become so focused on growing into someone that won't sabotage themselves for someone else that it's become uncomfortable to even entertain the thought of pouring into another person.

    The only exception will be the girl I've mentioned before, but there's so much distance between us now that I've lost hope in it all. In my eyes, it's so hard to let go because I want to show her what I've made of myself and how much I've grown since August 11th, 2020. As innocent as my intentions are, it can still be classified as remnants of an obsession because I'm obviously still holding on. I get engulfed in fantasizing about catching up and getting that "closure" we never got to have. Followed by kissing her on the forehead and telling her, "oh, how I've missed you, sunshine." Whenever I imagine it, my heart sheds another tear, and each one hurts as equally as the last.

    I'm writing this sincerely sorry that I don't have the answers you're looking for in this chapter, for the simple fact that I'm still going through the whole process myself. I've been reading *The Five Love Languages* by Gary Chapman, as well as numerous amounts of other books I will list for you, to gain a better understanding of the unique ways people need to be loved based on what they've gone through. I study and apply it to the platonic connections I have, yet I'm still super intimidated to really give myself another chance at intimacy. No amount of therapy, journaling, meditation, or exercise erases the memory of losing the love I once thought would be forever, all because I wasn't a healthy version of myself at the time. It really sucks.

That's why I've become so overly dedicated to my craft. It's become my primary source of happiness and the ONLY distraction that helps me keep my mind off of what once was. When it comes to love, I'm probably not the person to be giving advice as of right now, and that's okay with me. To know what healthy love is, I guess I had to understand what unhealthy love is as well. So here I am with a temporarily broken smile. I hope this therapy session was informative enough for you to not embarrass yourself like I have. The love you experience is an extension of the love you already have for yourself. If you're scared like me, then trust me; I'm especially rooting for your happiness.

One day, I know I will find the love I've always craved and desired with a woman. We'll get married, have a family, travel the globe, and uplift the community together as a unit. When that day comes, and you see that smile on my face, I want you to remember this moment. That way, you'll understand what it took for me to smile like I do. We all will, in our own timing. Until then, let's continue to pour our love back into ourselves because you are the one person that'll always be worth it. I promise you.

AGAIN, I'M SORRY I DON'T HAVE YOUR ANSWERS HERE. LET ME BE HUMAN TOO. I NEED TO FIND THE ANSWERS MYSELF FIRST, BUT LET ME KNOW IF YOU FIND THEM BEFORE ME! I NEED HELP TOO!

Recap: Don't love someone else more than you love yourself. Make sure you don't overextend yourself for people who won't even pour back into you. Know your worth and stand on it. Being in love is overrated. True unconditional love is where it's at.

Chapter Nine

Journaling Topic Question: In what ways do I experience love on a day-to-day basis? How can I embody the love I wish to attract?

PRIORITIES

"Too many people spend money they earned... to buy things they don't want... to impress people they don't like." - Will Rogers

Ahhh, the quote of the century. How many of you own an excessive number of things that you could honestly die without? Shoes, purses, action figures, even exotic drugs. Almost everyone is subject to wanting to flex on everyone else; there's no need to fight it! This is something all of our egos can get consumed by, something I like to call our Apex complex. It's always been the cool thing for people to be like, "I got what you want but don't have; I know you wish you were me." Honestly, it's a mental illness; why would anyone want something for the sole purpose of bragging to somebody who actually likes and appreciates it?

Well, to keep it simple and general, it boils down to our ego wanting to feel like it's superior. Why else would we put so much value in such frivolous things? The simple thought of obtaining what the collective desires makes us feel as if we're magically better than anyone who doesn't have it. Even if we don't personally resonate with the item, there are still people that'll brag about it because they know others will be jealous. Some even do it in an attempt to get attention from people they desire to be around. Either way, we can believe it's an instant ticket into the "in" crowd, and that's the reason we gravitate towards it! This principle is, unfortunately, a base code chiseled into our DNA.

As much as I'd like to deny it (especially for myself), we are constantly being influenced to "fit in" with the collective. There's something about being a part of something bigger than the individual that really fills us with contentment. Now I could have talked about this in the chapter about being aware of the company you keep around you, but this is less about the company you keep and more about how YOU interact with the company. There's nothing existentially wrong with being around people that don't completely align with what you want out of life (family, coworkers, neighbors) as long as you establish the proper boundaries for yourself. If they're slacking off on productivity and encourage you to join them, it's up to you to either clear your busy schedule and make them happy, or prioritize what matters to you.

    I bring this up because the same applies to our desire to reach the top of the financial pyramid. People are either constantly working towards leveling up organically or putting up a facade that they're always at the top. Especially with social media being the major trend now, it gives people the opportunity to paint a pretty picture for the audience. Our desire to flex on everyone else and our insecurities about what we don't possess has never been exploited more. It's led to even more people constantly looking over the fence to see how green their grass is compared to their neighbor's. They will even buy the latest exclusive drops just because everyone else is talking about it, even if it isn't the responsible thing to do. I've witnessed people spend all their money on top-shelf drugs, clothes, shoes, and vacations when they have legitimate responsibilities that their funds should be going towards. People will have kids that need more clothes, snacks, and toys, and they will still buy some Percocet because their favorite rapper said so. All because they saw how happy the next person was to have it! Especially how envious everyone else was about it, it's crazy!

Again, I'd like to confess that I was no exception to this! Before the events that inspired me to write this, I did everything I could to keep up with impressing everyone around me. Instead of saving up the little income I was making, I screamed *fuck it*! I bought any and everything my then-girlfriend wanted in an attempt to keep a smile on her face. I constantly went out to party and eat out with my friends when there were bills I could've helped my family with. Every time I experienced something others would be envious about, you're damn right I made sure I posted it on my Instagram story!

It was only when I saw these people weren't really happy for me that I realized how important it was to prioritize what matters to me. What makes ME happy. What inspires ME to jump out of bed and rise to the occasion every single day. That's when it became crystal clear how essential it was to not even ponder on what's on the other side of the fence. My grass doesn't rely on theirs, and their grass doesn't rely on mine! In the wise words of Jermaine Cole, "What you eat don't make me shit, and who you fuck don't make me cum."

    Since then, I've made it my sole responsibility to do what resonates with me and the future I've dreamt of creating. Looking back on it, I can admit that some of the things I experienced or possessed were things I thoroughly enjoyed, but in no way were they important enough to prioritize over achieving my goals. It wasn't until I was able to step out of the situation that I realized how much time and energy I was spending on them. I've always had ideas for books, movies, tv shows, vlogs, applications, institutions, and so much more. I have my eyes set on becoming my generation's next Walt Disney or Steve Jobs, and it wasn't like I didn't know that. In order to see these seeds come into fruition, I had to fully commit not just a period of my time but my entire life force to it, no matter how unorthodox or lonely it would feel. Actually, I think it was the very fact that I was aware of how big of a commitment these dreams required that I was intimidated into prioritizing other's wants and needs over my own. My dreams required so much of a commitment that it seemed intangible! And to stop me from contemplating about how nearly impossible it was to achieve, I resorted to distracting myself (I think we all know how that turned out by now).

    The point is, if you have goals and deadlines that are significant to you and your aspirations, make sure you treat them with the respect they deserve. Don't lose sight of what's important while trying to impress other people. Find the willpower and discipline to stick to your own values so that when you reach your happiness, nobody can take that away from you. Even if the road is the one less traveled, if that's what resonates with your soul, then go for it at full speed! Don't EVER let the trend convince you that it's worth more than long-term contentment. Trends are usually short-lived anyways.

    Don't ever get intimidated from realizing how much dedication it'll take to achieve the things you want. I learned firsthand that the size of the goal will dictate how great of commitment you must make to achieve it. So when I say I had goals of influencing positive change in this world through multiple art forms, the commitment required was more massive than the average person can handle/maintain. The main reasons why I pushed through it were simple; I knew without a doubt in my mind that I was far from average, and I knew there was nothing else on this 3D plane that interested me more. So, in my case, I had two choices; either stop entertaining lower frequencies and focus on building a healthier community, or find false happiness in a life that I wasn't living to my full potential. Which one do you think you would pick?

Since I was a child, I've always loved Spiderman. From the costume, to his powers, to being able to swing around the city while saving the world, he's always been one of my inspirations! For all my other Spidey-fanatics, you probably know what I'm about to quote before I even write it.

"With great power comes great responsibility."

Chapter Ten

It's unfortunate that Uncle Ben met his fate shortly after saying this, but it's honestly the most grounding mantra for anyone to remember throughout their life, especially someone like Spiderman. By this part of the book and your journaling, I hope that you've made phenomenal progress transitioning from doubting your true potential into realizing that you hold all the power you've always fantasized about having. If you haven't noticed already, the biggest thing restricting you from tapping into that potential is the lack of prioritizing what feeds your power over what feeds your fear. How many times did Peter Parker have to cancel his dream chance with Mary Jane just because the world needed his help? If he chose to neglect his top priority of keeping everyone safe and took a real shot at living out his love life, there wouldn't be a world left for him to love in!

We could all be our own superheroes, as well as our own worst enemies. It all depends on what thoughts, habits, and attention we feed into that will clearly define what role we're playing for ourselves. Our Creator instilled in us the power of being the co-creators of our very own experience on this Earth. We all have a primary soul desire, and the Universe will guide us towards it as long as we're doing our part to create the supporting details so that "main idea" isn't just that; an idea. It's all about prioritizing your diet! As long as we don't waver to the pleasures outside our goals, each and every day will feel one step closer to what we want. The main obstacle is establishing that top priority and sticking to it, because whether it's to be a millionaire, a neighborhood baker, a stripper, a gypsy, or even someone living on the streets, this Universe will work its magic to manifest whatever it is you prioritize! That's why you always have to be mindful that what you're doing aligns with what you want to build for yourself.

Uncle Ben's Wisdom

There's no need to sugarcoat this. I think both of us can agree that if you don't have a grasp of what your ideal priorities are already, then it'll be wise to go over what I wrote in the "Diet" section. I made this a whole chapter instead of building onto that one because, to put it in the simplest terms, this is the advanced section. Understanding who you are, what should be a part of your diet, who should be a part of the company you keep around, and the patience necessary to get it down are the foundations of your success. These things should be established before this phase. However, just like knowing how to diffuse a bomb can be beneficial, it's kind of meaningless if you don't apply it. You know the lesson already, now it's time for practice!

Since you've started reading this book, have you put a conscious effort into applying what we've learned? As much as I want to hold you accountable and slap you across the face if your answer is no, in your reality, I'm only words on a paper. I can't babysit or mentor you in the ways that I do for myself (quite honestly, I have a hard time doing that at times too). That responsibility falls in your hands and yours alone.

The only person who has the real power to change your life and sustain it is you, my friend. You can have family, friends, even licensed professionals there to help you, but that's all they are, help. If you need a slap in the face for a reality check that'll get you back on track, you're going to have to do it yourself.

You need to be able to commit to your plan in order to see the results you want, and for that, you'll have to constantly put new progress over your old pleasures. You can go out all you want! Drink until you sound like a cartoon character, fuck the most beautiful people that walk this planet, even play *Fortnite* when you have a big test the next day. All of these things are okay! But will you be okay with the consequences of your actions? You just have to remember that at the end of the day, you'll be the one that will have to deal with the consequences, whether they be good or bad.

I'm trying to get you to realize that we're constantly choosing what life we want to live, and I want all of us to choose our highest timeline. Settling for one lower than our full potential isn't necessarily a bad thing; it simply means that you settled. My TOP priority is to become my best self so that I can tell everyone that it might be okay for others to settle, but not you! The fact that you picked up this book, let

Chapter Ten

alone got this far, is all the proof we need to know that you are one of the chosen individuals to raise this world's vibrations. I'm not asking you; I'm reassuring you. All that needs to be done is reevaluating what you prioritize.

You have all the power you need! You don't need to keep hearing me repeat myself if you already believed it. The most popular way people give away that power is by not keeping their priorities in check. You MUST hold yourself accountable for the future you create. It's no one else's fault if you want to be in the NBA, yet you spend more time playing NBA 2K with your friends than you do practicing your jump shot so you can make the high school team. Just like it would've been no one else's fault if I wanted to write a book, yet I spent more time talking about it than actually writing it. It was up to me to change my life.

If I didn't want to buckle down and stick to my recipe to get my company established, then I probably would've convinced myself that what I dreamed of couldn't be done. But if that was the case, I would've never felt this fulfillment of purpose I'm feeling as I'm writing the finals pages. I would've never got myself to write out my thoughts in such a way that might actually help someone else through their own obstacles. It's because I stuck to what mattered to me that I'm able to do all of these things, and that's what I want for you. That's what you should want for yourself. Fuck what everyone else wants. From this point on, this is about YOU. That's how you'll be able to unlock the next chapter of your own story. Who knows, maybe you'll end up being the person I end up passing the torch to when the time comes! Just keep working.

Recap: Fill in the blanks. Don't make me repeat myself. THIS IS THE ADVANCED SECTION. Go back and read if you need to.

Journaling Topic Question: How do I self-define success? How are my actions in alignment with that belief? Am I really making the progress I intended? Am I really spending my time efficiently?

Chapter Eleven

YOU

"It's better to prepare for an opportunity and not have one, than to have an opportunity and not be prepared." - Whitney M. Young Jr.

At last! We've come not to the end of the road, but the end of these pages. The *REAL challenge* is applying what we've learned on this journey and truly making the best out of every day we have. That's where I'm at in my life now. The purpose of writing my thoughts out like this was to acknowledge that there's room for improvement within myself and inspire you to do the same in your own way. As you can tell by now, these topics aren't something out of the ordinary, and it's clear I haven't found the solution to these topics and wrote it all down; I'm merely accepting that certain aspects exist within me. This was all an exercise to challenge the extent of my self-awareness.

Looking back on it, the steps I took to battling each chapter are pretty similar to tactics found at AA meetings (I guess they know what they're doing in there). I can break down the framework for you, but, well, you're literally reading the last chapter of the book, so don't make me do it. If you didn't catch the pattern as I tackled each topic, I strongly suggest, at the very least, you do your own research on it. Read it, study it, learn it, and then apply it to any aspect of life where you want more (or just different) results. You don't need to follow the steps I took to conquer my own issues; the fact that they helped me does not guarantee your success. You've only been reading the process of me learning more about myself to comprehend what's next. In order to conquer thy enemy, thou must know thy enemy (or toxic trait or habit or whatever); and in your case, it's you.

Now what I'm about to say is important; all of my words are preparation for creating the desired success we've dreamt of. This is MY STORY. This is NOT, and I repeat NOT, a sure-fire way to instantly manifest said opportunity into your life. I think we can all agree that we have no control over the external circumstances in this world, like if the audience personally likes your performance or if people react positively to the book you wrote. The only things we have control over are our individual vessels' movements, the words we speak, and applying wisdom from our past experiences. As much as we capitalize on the things in our control, it doesn't have absolute power over the way everything plays out.

If you went through this journey and came out a whole new and improved version of yourself, but that person you wanted to share it with has moved on, it's okay! I'll agree with you that it sounds like bullshit to say that, but trust me, it's okay. Remember? I've been going through the same journey as I wrote this! When I say it's okay, I'm speaking from a place of experience. At the very least, we've gone through a metamorphosis to intentionally enhance the qualities of our lives. If that person is stuck on the past you, fuck em! We are no longer defined by who we once were, so in the end, you still come out as a winner. They willingly choose to opt out of experiencing the best, healthiest version of you, and all that means is that there's another opportunity that'll align with the connection meant for you. Remember! You're both the prize and the competitor! The only competition is the past versions of yourself.

When I started this book, I booked a flight to move to San Francisco the day after my 25th birthday, three months from when I began writing. I was in the throes of a crippling depression, both mentally and physically, but I knew that wasn't how I wanted to live my life. I knew it was time to travel the world and live out my dreams instead of just planning and fantasizing about them. The only thing that was in the way of me not jumping the gun and flying out instantly was that I needed proper preparation, like I've said before. I knew that as much as I wanted my dreams to materialize and to seize every opportunity that came my way, it would be meaningless if I wasn't really ready for it.

I could have easily fumbled a great opportunity because I didn't know how to handle it, but luckily (and equally unluckily), I was familiar with opportunities not being handled correctly. Everything that I ever wanted was on its way to me! It was my wisdom of mishandling it because I wanted to rush it that helped me acknowledge the fact that my outdated pattern would only fill me with more regret than postponing it for a time when I know I can step up to the plate.

    With indescribable happiness, I can say that I'm now writing this on January 4th, 2021, currently over the Gulf of Mexico on my way to a whole new state. The emotions I've felt and gone through in the past three months, let alone the past three days, have been a growing experience I wasn't quite braced for. I've kept my head down and dived deep into my shadow work for so long that when it was time for me to leave, I looked up and couldn't believe the growth I obtained over time. Since I began this journey, I felt like this day would never come. In between my goal and my past self were massive amounts of self-work and over two thousand hours of patience. How did I get through it? More simply put than done, I had to detach from the results and fall in love with the process.

    I had to continuously trick myself into believing things like reading, meditating, learning, cooking, journaling, laundry, hygiene, and writing a book was FUN. Watching TV? If it doesn't exercise my critical thinking, what's the point? Hanging out with people and doing absolutely nothing? Blasphemy! We're either building on established plans or creating new ones. I had to theoretically rewire my circuits if I want to stop practicing insanity. To live in the elevated state of being that I strived for, I needed to change the way I spent my time. I needed to PREPARE.

A close friend of mine (and the one who helped with each journaling question) always preaches about how our attention is one of the most valuable things we can give. The definition of attention is "The act or the power of fixing the mind on something," so in other words, it's literally what your brain is focused on. Whether it's a game, work, sex, TV, money, family, nature, exercise, or mediation, this is what you're investing your time and energy in, like it or not. Sounding familiar?

We can even build on the student analogy I used earlier. They could watch their professor's lectures countless times, but if they find themselves having sexual fantasies instead of listening to what the professor is actually saying, then it's just a waste of time. Don't get confused; they're in the right place! They have everything they need to succeed in front of them. It's just that they didn't see the importance of intentional attention instead of just showing up physically, and that's the whole point I want to get across here. It's one thing to make sure you're at the right place at the right time. It's another to not let that moment pass you by.

Just like you reading this book. You can be someone who wants to become the best version of yourself, and that's what I want for you! I've tried my best to address factors of mental blocks and instabilities and be vulnerable enough to share a lot of my low points to embrace them as the catalyst of my metamorphosis. All to help people embrace their own shortcomings. But, hypothetically, if you've been reading this with the simple intentions of just hearing about my imperfections to judge who I am, then your misdirected attention could have distracted you from the opportunity this book serves in your life.

Luckily for all of us, this isn't a lecture I have to repeat over and over again. These words were meant to be there when we need them and put down when we want. This was the opportunity I created for us as I prepare for the goals I'm pursuing after this phase of life. The thing is, I knew I wasn't the best version of myself while being locked up in the house, and I refused to let that situation make me fumble my future bags.

To be honest, I'm still in awe that I've been able to incorporate my personal goals into my life's work. I'm so grateful that I've been able to push through my fears and pour my soul onto center stage with such unshakable awareness and confidence in who I am and what has made me the person I am today. This is the strength I intentionally aimed to achieve after completing this, and here I am now at the top of the mountain I once called my obstacles.

As discouraged as I felt through it all, I wanted to share my whole process of dealing with my skeletons because it was the most effective way to

Chapter Eleven

inspire my audience to deal with theirs. I didn't do this to narcissistically sell you my problems in a packaged diary. The fact that we are all human beings made from the same source is reason enough for me to believe that people go through the same things I do. So please, *please* don't miss a special opportunity created uniquely for you because merely witnessing my journey is much easier than taking your own. Do the work as if the version of me in the past chapters is growing with you.

At this point in my life, I can relish in the life I've been manifesting since I started this commitment. I'm not saying I've reached my "paradise," I'm saying I've reached the top of this mountain. From what I can see, there's plenty more to climb. In theory, everything starts and ends with you. You are the creator of what you desire, which directly correlates with how you play your role as co-creator in the collective. So, continue to dream! What rises must fall so it may rise again. Whenever you feel yourself falling, embrace the beauty of it and know that when it's time for your new opportunity, you're ready. You've always been ready. It's your birthright to live in your highest timeline, just like it's mine or anyone else's. Keep working, my dear friend. One day, you'll see the fruits of your labor. Until then, be kind, be well, and be yourself. And so, it is written.

With much love,

Brandon Azeem.

Chapter Eleven

RESOURCES

My story is heavily influenced by pop culture! From books, to movies, shows, motivational videos, interviews, and everything else I've indulged in up until this point, I found myself paraphrasing life itself to find my authentic way of explaining these topics. If I've left you or your work out of this list I humbly apologize! It is not my intentions to leave you out. I, uh, am a pretty forgetful stoner, but I tried REALLY hard to make sure nobody was left out! If I DID (again, I'm sorry) please reach out! This is only the first edition of this book, so give me the chance to add you to the next one! Thank you so much for reading!

- Oh, the Places You'll Go! by Dr. Seuss
- You are A Badass by Jen Sincero
- Dora The Explorer by Chris Gifford/Nickelodeon
- The Alchemist by Paulo Coelho
- Avengers: Infinity War by Marvel/Disney
- Super Mario 64 by Nintendo
- Soul by Pixar & Disney

Resources

- Finding Nemo by Pixar & Disney
- Unfuck Yourself by Gary John Bishop
- The Subtle Art of Not Giving A Fuck by Mark Manson
- Everything is Fucked by Mark Manson
- The Five Love Languages by Gary Chapman
- The Seven Spiritual Laws of Success by Deepak Chopra
- What Got You Here Won't Get You There by Marshall Goldsmith
- The Way of the Superior Man by David Deida
- The Power of Now by Eckhart Tolle
- A Series of Unfortunate Events by Lemony Snicket
- The Percy Jackson & The Olympians Series by Rick Riordan
- In & Of Itself by Derek Delgaudio
- Spider-Man by Sony/Marvel
- Spiderman Video Game by Sony/Marvel
- Lalilaluna TV (Jazmin Kylene)

Again, if I forgot anyone or anything, reach out! This is my story in my own words, but I grab my inspiration from everyday life. I would hate that someone/something didn't get the credit that it rightfully deserves.

EPILOGUE

Today's the day I reached the top of the mountain. I'd say the view was worth the journey, but I'm too tired to stand up and see it. The taste of victory is sweet, but it lost its flavor. The people I would turn to are no longer on the same path as me. I thought this is what I wanted. I thought walking every step of the way would help me be content with whatever was waiting for me at the finish line, but here I am.

In front of me is yet another fork in the road. To my left, there's plenty of land to explore with what looks like a skyline in the distance? I'm thinking that can be a chance to restock on supplies, maybe even be someplace I wouldn't mind settling down at. The biggest problem is there's no safe way down. The slants are too steep to stop myself from slipping off the cliffs, and by the time I go back the way I came

Epilogue

and walk around, I'd already have died from starvation.

    To the right of me is what I really have my eyes set on. Across the sea is another peak that I wish to stand on top of, but there's no land between my position and destination. I'd take a boat, but the only one in sight looks like it's already on its way there now, so there's my luck. If only swimming was an option, I'd jump in and start going now. But just to further discourage me, the height of my dive might just kill me. And if that doesn't, then I'm sure the sea monsters will have a blast knowing I'm on their turf. So, looks like I'm a sitting duck.

    My food and water supplies have been completely diminished on my climb up, but there's no way I'm dying here. There are a few plants with a few bulbs blooming, but these don't naturally grow in this climate. Did somebody start a garden? Now that I think of it, why is there a paved road that leads all the way to the mountain top? Does someone live here?

Baz Tha Nomad's Paradise Parkway

All that's up here is a burnt-out campfire and this weird jet-black tent with sigils on both sides to complete this oddly placed campsite. Bizarre, right? I thought I was the only one who knew about this spot. If someone's been up here long enough to set up shop, then maybe they know how to help me! That's probably a long shot, but I made it this far! Now it's the time for the waiting game...

It's been hours and still no sign of another life form. There seems to be a light-emitting from inside the tent, but whenever I called out to check for a response or just a sign that it's safe for me to enter, there's no answer. The winds are blowing so violently that they may be stealing the sound of my voice before it even reaches, so I should just walk in, right? The Sun's going down soon, and if I don't do this now, I'm afraid whoever lives here is going to find a carcass to feed their next fire. It's either get up now or start burning these pages.

Considering the fact that my clothes are now

Epilogue

covered with dirt and filth to the point where it looks like I've been rolling in manure, my beard and hair combination makes me resemble someone trying out for a *Castaway* sequel, and my social skills are on par with a prisoner fresh out of solitary confinement, it's safe to say that I'm probably walking into my own demise. I can see the headlines now; "Thug dies while trying to attack local camper." The odds of me surviving are slim to none, but it's looking like the only chance for me to get to where I want to go. I've made it this far, and I'd be damned if this is as far as I get.

Who knows? Maybe they'll end up being happy to see another human and offer me all the things I need. Maybe they hold the wisdom I'm seeking to aid my journey. Maybe they're the best chef this world has ever known and came up here to harvest their special ingredient. I'm so afraid of what's on the other side of that tent that I forgot to consider the chance that maybe, that person is someone just like me. Maybe it'll be such a great time I don't ever want to leave. The possibilities are endless; I just won't know until I find out.

    Okay. Here I go, wish me luck! I'll update you as soon as I can.

Next

Psychosis Cave

www.ingramcontent.com/pod-product-compliance
Lightning Source LLC
LaVergne TN
LVHW090116080426
835507LV00040B/905